MOVIE MAGIC
in the Classroom

Movies belong in the curriculum—and not just the day before a holiday. This book by award-winning educator Amber Chandler shows why films are so important for teaching social emotional learning and critical thinking. She provides complete guides to ten current, age-appropriate movies; each guide features a pre-viewing activity, a stop-and-chat guide for you so you know when to pause for discussion, a student notes sheet, and discussion questions with varying formats. The book also offers handy tools such as blank templates and permissions forms for communication with parents. Every movie addresses some aspects of CASEL's SEL Competencies: Self-Awareness, Self-Management, Responsible Decision-Making, Relationship Skills, and Social Awareness. Amber Chandler does all the prep work for you, so you can lean into the movie experience and share this opportunity with your students, putting movie magic to work!

Amber Chandler is a National Board Certified middle school English language arts (ELA) teacher in Hamburg, New York, and an adjunct professor at Canisius College in Buffalo, New York. No matter which level Chandler is teaching, the goal is always the same: to enable students to take charge of their own learning. Chandler's website, flexibleclass.com, has many resources to support teachers, and she regularly updates lessons and provides links to her webinars. Follow her on Twitter @MsAmberChandler and check out more than 300 of her free resources on ShareMyLesson.com.

Also Available from Amber Chandler
(www.routledge.com/k-12)

The Flexible SEL Classroom, Second Edition:
Practical Ways to Build Social Emotional Learning

The Flexible ELA Classroom:
Practical Tools for Differentiated Instruction in Grades 4–8

MOVIE MAGIC
in the Classroom

Ready-to-Use Guide for
Teaching SEL

Amber Chandler

Routledge
Taylor & Francis Group

NEW YORK AND LONDON

Cover image: © Getty Images

First published 2023
by Routledge
605 Third Avenue, New York, NY 10158

and by Routledge
4 Park Square, Milton Park, Abingdon, Oxon, OX14 4RN

Routledge is an imprint of the Taylor & Francis Group, an informa business

Library of Congress Cataloging-in-Publication Data
Names: Chandler, Amber, author.
Title: Movie magic in the classroom : Ready-to-Use Guide for
    Teaching SEL / Amber Chandler.
Description: New York, NY : Routledge, 2023. | Includes bibliographical references.
Identifiers: LCCN 2022022297 | ISBN 9781032294841 (hardback) |
    ISBN 9781032281575 (paperback) | ISBN 9781003301790 (ebook)
Subjects: LCSH: Motion pictures in education. | Affective education—Audio-visual aids.
Classification: LCC LB1044 .C473 2023 | DDC 371.33/523—dc23/eng/20220713
LC record available at https://lccn.loc.gov/2022022297

ISBN: 978-1-032-29484-1 (hbk)
ISBN: 978-1-032-28157-5 (pbk)
ISBN: 978-1-003-30179-0 (ebk)

DOI: 10.4324/9781003301790

Typeset in Warnock Pro
by Apex CoVantage, LLC

You can access the Support material at: www.routledge.com/9781032281575

For my Matty, my movie buddy for over two decades. I love you and appreciate all the ways you support me, us, and our family.

Contents

Contents

Support Material

The handouts in each chapter and in the appendix are also available as free downloads on our website, so you can easily print them for classroom use.

You can access these downloads by visiting the book product page: www.routledge.com/9781032281575. Click on the tab that says "Support Material" and select the files. They will begin downloading to your computer.

Meet the Author

Amber Chandler is a National Board Certified middle school ELA teacher in Hamburg, New York with a Master's Degree in Literature, as well as a School District Leader certification. She was the 2018 AMLE Educator of the Year and a 2022 New York State Teacher of the Year finalist. Amber has enjoyed a wide variety of teaching opportunities. Amber is an eighth grade middle school ELA teacher, as well as an adjunct professor at Canisius College. No matter which level Amber is teaching, the goal is always the same: engage students to take charge of their own learning.

Amber's blogs and articles have appeared in MiddleWeb, ShareMyLesson, Getting Smart, ASCD's "Ideas From the Field," Mom's Rising, The EdVocate, *AMLE Magazine*, as well as *New York Teacher*. Amber's blogs and webinars for AFT's ShareMyLesson have repeatedly been in the top of the year, and several in the top five of the decade. Amber enjoys speaking about student engagement, Project Based Learning, and SEL, at AFT TEACH, the AMLE annual conference, and Learning and the Brain conferences.

Amber was chosen from a nationwide search as one of a handful of panelists for Fordham's "Evaluating the Content and Quality of Next Generation Assessments" to evaluate how state assessments compare in their ability to assess Common Core Standards. She's also served as a School Review Team member, offering her observations and expertise, particularly in the area of Project Based Learning.

Amber is an SEL Consultant for Capstone Publisher's "My Spectacular Self" series, as well as for the GoPebble! Division. She provides SEL questions for student engagement, as well as offering developmentally appropriate advice to parents.

Amber is an active AFT member as a ShareMyLesson Partner and participant in the Resource and Materials Development at the Summer

Educators Academy. Amber recently served on NYSUT's "Future Forward Taskforce" as a voice for SEL initiatives as schools return to in-person, post-pandemic instruction. She serves as the President for her local Frontier Central Teachers Association.

Amber's website, flexibleclass.com, has many resources to support teachers, and she regularly updates lessons and provides links to her webinars. Follow her on Twitter @MsAmberChandler, and check out more than 300 of her free resources on ShareMyLesson.com.

Preface

Back in 2017, I sat in the warm movie theater with my family, watching *Zootopia*. Within the first five minutes of the movie, I leaned over and whispered to my daughter, "I'm going to teach this!" I had been looking for a way to broach social justice issues with my middle school students, and this movie was going to be my way in—a way to have meaningful conversations that were developmentally appropriate, yet dealt with racism, sexism, bias, and the importance of a global worldview. Flashforward to the end of 2017 when ShareMyLesson announced that my *Zootopia* lesson was the #1 Top Lesson of 2017 and the blog about this lesson was the #2 Blog of the Decade, and #2 Blog of 2017. It's nearing 5,000 downloads. The lesson is featured in *The Flexible SEL Classroom*, and I am extremely proud of it.

Little did I know that the "important conversations" I needed to have with my students would reach new heights. In March of 2020, the COVID pandemic hit, and the political divide in our country became volatile as the summer of 2020 heated up. What started out as an inconvenience two years ago has clearly turned into a life-defining event for so many of our students and families. Teachers are struggling to help students who are experiencing the trauma of several years of uncertainty, disrupted schooling, isolation, and a looming enemy that keeps mutating. I decided that it was time to update *The Flexible SEL Classroom* to try to touch upon some "Pandemic Principles" that might help educators reach struggling students. I added a chapter on Resilience and one on Restorative Circles. As I prepared the new book, I was sitting in the movies again, this time watching *Cruella*, and again, I leaned across to my daughter and whispered, "I'm going to teach this!" *Cruella* was added to the new edition, and it was just named the #2 Partner Lesson of 2021 with nearly 1,000 downloads in only a handful of months, since I didn't post it until the fall.

Updating *The Flexible SEL Classroom* was exciting, and once I was building a unit around yet another movie, it occurred to me that movies are vehicles for the important conversations we need to be having with our students right now. I started bouncing the idea off colleagues, asking them what movies they'd teach if they had "ready-to-go" plans for pre-viewing, viewing, post-viewing discussions, and a Stop and Chat. What movies could be utilized to teach social justice issues, reinforce social and emotional learning, and build upon universally important speaking, listening, and viewing skills?

What you'll find in this book are ten movies that "made the cut." As the mom of a middle schooler and a high schooler, I had the perfect vetters right here at home. These are the movies that both teens agreed they'd like to watch at school, in a mixed audience of their peers, taught by their current teachers. I add this caveat because there are some amazing movies that I'd love to teach, but I don't necessarily think would work for all students in a school setting. The book is sorted by rating, with PG being appropriate for middle or high school students, and the PG-13 being more at your discretion based on the culture and climate of your school and your willingness to "go there." The appendixes have a generic permission slip you may use, an alternate assignment in case parents opt out of the movie you choose, and an assessment choice board that is applicable to any movie.

Each chapter contains a pre-viewing activity that acts as your "hook" or "activator." There is a note sheet for students to use during the viewing, as well as a post-viewing discussion guide. The Teacher Stop and Chat gives the timestamps to direct you when to pause for discussion with social and emotional connections, as well as cool facts or interesting cross-curricular notes. The book can be used to teach an entire film course with social emotional learning, used with an advisory period, or even left as a long-term sub plan for a few weeks' absence. Each unit can be done within a week or so, or used as the basis for further writing and projects that you can find on the choice board. Ultimately, as with all the resources I share with educators, there's a tremendous amount of flexibility. My hope is that you'll be able to use these templates to bring *Movie Magic* into your classroom while using the opportunity to enhance social and emotional learning for your students. Enjoy the movie! (There's still time to grab popcorn. . . .)

Introduction

For as long as I can remember, movies have been a vital part of my story. If that sounds overblown, let me explain. "My story" begins, I suppose, in fifth grade, with staying up late in my parents' living room, sprawled on a late 70s staple: a velour-like plaid couch with tasseled trim at the bottom. For some reason, and I really can't come up with a good one, my parents let me stay up on Friday nights and watch television after they went to bed. This was an independence that I can't imagine making sense for a fifth grader, but then I think of all the screens kiddos have nowadays constantly accessible, and my wild freedom seems antiquated. No matter; trust me when I tell you that I took Friday nights very seriously. I'd make popcorn in our air popper, which was a really big deal at the time—both that we were cool enough to have one and that I was able to operate it alone. I'd make sure I had a notebook handy as well. Once everyone had settled in, I would go to the HBO channel and find a movie to watch. This is my story: *I wasn't watching television. I was watching the Home Box Office channel where I could watch movies. In my house.*

Wait, you might be thinking. How is that a vital part of your story? In those stolen moments alone I was given access to the world outside of my own. My own world was small and safe, and ever so provincial: a house in the suburbs with a stay-at-home mom, a dad who traveled three days a week, four siblings, a small elementary school, and an overprotected existence due to my dad's reckless upbringing and my mom's need to keep the three youngest of us safe and in the same room at the same time, lest we destroy all the rooms of the house, not just one. I marvel at how little I remember talking with my parents when I was little. We didn't discuss things. It was the times; children were seen not heard, maybe, or it could have just been my family. It is impossible to determine what was common or uncommon about your childhood while you are in it since you have so little fodder for comparison. I didn't miss my parents discussing things with me, but I did know that other than the indistinct clatter of lots of children, there weren't a whole lot of true conversations in my house. I felt an emptiness that I could not name and still have a hard time deciphering. I think what I was missing was connection.

My parents never once asked what I watched, nor did they give me any direction about what I could and couldn't watch. I knew they would not approve of an "R"-rated movie. My mom didn't even watch them, but I put all thought of their approval out of my head and just didn't entertain thoughts of them at all. On that couch late into Friday nights, I was my own person, no one's child. It was 1985, and I was learning how to interpret my inner monologue by channeling other voices, connecting me to a greater outside world.

I watched scary movies—*Cat's Eye* and *Day of the Dead* stand out to me, and I still like a good psychological thriller and occasional apocalyptic nightmare. I watched comedies—*European Vacation*, *Real Genius*, and *Teen Wolf*. However, as an English teacher I'm ashamed to admit this: nothing, not even books, has had as big an impact on my intellectual world, moral compass, and creative life than movies. And, wow, the movies I watched in my formative years! Though wildly beyond my years in content, these movies were amazing: *The Color Purple*, *Out of Africa*, *A Room With a View*, *St. Elmo's Fire*, *My Life as a Dog*, *North and South*, *Death of a Salesman*, *The Falcon and the Snowman*—each week I was transfixed by the world outside of mine, and it gave me hope that one day I'd find that connection to a greater world. I scribbled down dialogue, notes, and quotes in my notebook.

If you aren't a movie fan, this may all sound melodramatic, but you probably wouldn't be reading this introduction if you weren't a bit like me. Movies have shared the world with me. I've connected to characters in ways that I don't often connect with people, and I've escaped the humdrum. I've learned lessons living vicariously that I'd never want to experience in real life.

It's interesting. I'm 48 years old, and many people my age bemoan the addiction of their children or students to screens, but I remember fondly the television of my youth. It was always on. Cartoons, soap operas, after-school specials, news, and my personal favorite: the mini-series. I'm not arguing that my family wouldn't have done better if they had turned off the television, but I am arguing that if they weren't going to do that, I was glad to have the familiar voices instead of silence.

Let's jump ahead to why you might have bought this book or are pondering doing so. You, like me, have a hunch that there's a really powerful way to help students with their social and emotional needs through movies. You love this idea, and every time you watch a movie you wonder if you could somehow incorporate it into your classroom. Yet—and here's how using movies in the classroom usually ends—you don't have time to figure out whole lessons, build activities, and so forth, so you allow a movie the day before a holiday or when you are unexpectedly absent. You know movies matter, but it isn't as if you have time to create something new for something that isn't in the curriculum.

This book is going to show you why movies belong in the curriculum and how to make the case for their inclusion in your programming, and it will provide you with ten movies to use, complete with a pre-viewing activity, as-you-view note sheets, a stop-and-chat guide for you so you know when to pause for discussion, discussion questions, and some ideas for assessment. Every movie addresses some aspects of CASEL's SEL Competencies: Self-Awareness, Self-Management, Responsible Decision-Making, Relationship Skills, and Social Awareness. Are these the only worthwhile movies? Definitely not. However, the work is done for you, and now you can lean into the movie experience and share this opportunity with your students, finally putting *Movie Magic* to work!

CHAPTER 1

Inside Out

Director: Pete Docter
Soul
Inside Out
Up!
Monsters, Inc.

Easter Eggs:
— Riley's yelling and screaming as a toddler is recycled from *Monsters, Inc.*'s character Boo (Docter is also the director of that film).
— Playground that is in Riley's Memory Orb might look familiar, as it is Sunnyside Daycare from *Toy Story 3*.

Music: Michael Giacchino
Zootopia
Rogue One
Call of Duty
Lost
Spider-Man
Coco
Jurassic World

Characters:
Riley: Kaitlyn Dias
Jill: Diane Lane
Bill: Kyle MacLachlan
Joy: Amy Poehler
Sadness: Phyllis Smith
Fear: Bill Hader
Disgust: Mindy Kaling
Anger: Lewis Black

DOI: 10.4324/9781003301790-1

When I pitched this book, I knew my biggest task would be to narrow down the list of movies that I could write about. First, they'd need to be school-appropriate; second, they'd need to provide the social and emotional lessons that kiddos desperately need. Finally, there'd have to be an intangible quality to the movies, one that guaranteed me that this movie would "age well." You'll notice that some of these movies are older, and it is that intangible quality that will allow generation after generation to enjoy and learn from them. The first movie is the gold standard for movies that hit all these criteria. *Inside Out* is the quintessential movie that is ready to impact your classroom socially and emotionally, which will, in turn, impact the academic side of things.

Though *Inside Out* is about Riley, an 11-year-old girl, the message is easily transferable to all students. Riley is a gender-neutral name, and Riley's emotions are depicted as both male and female, while the other characters' emotions are gender-specific. The extent to which these directorial choices are addressed is entirely up to the teacher, but it is worth noting that this protagonist is meant to be a bit of all of us, no matter our age or gender identity.

The central conflict of the story is Riley's move from the Midwest to San Francisco. While this is obviously a physical move, it can also be discussed in terms of adolescence. We use the language of physical location all the time to discuss students' ability to "fit in" and "find your place." There is nothing quite as disconcerting as the transformations of adolescence, and I've watched year after year as students "move" from one type of student into another, as conspicuous as any physical move. In a very real way, all adolescence is a dramatic move from one state of being to another.

Let's take Greg as an example. Greg was a little overweight, a cutie with dimples, and his parents definitely bought his back-to-school eighth-grade outfits from JCPenney endcaps, making him seem like a politically correct advertisement for middle America. He began eighth grade extremely quiet, arriving to my class each day a little late. He'd reluctantly take his seat, and never make eye contact with anyone. When he failed a quiz in October that he'd not prepared for, he welled up, and I called his dad to warn him that his son was very upset.

Flash forward three months. Greg had found a group who wore black eyeliner and dark lipstick and used they/them pronouns. These kiddos were open-minded, and frankly, they provided an escape that Greg needed from toxic middle school masculinity that had been judging him harshly based on his lack of athleticism and ability to hurl a well-timed insult. These kiddos listened to sad songs and sketched, made each other bracelets, and walked arm in arm to class. Greg came back from winter break with black, long-sleeved t-shirts, jeans with a chain belt, and black-checkered Vans. He wore a little eyeliner, but in a way that indicated that he might have applied it at lunch, not at home. I expected he'd wash it off before he caught the bus home. If I were to use a metaphor for this transformation, it would be one of moving—inhabiting a different terrain. Greg, surely, was still himself underneath, but his exterior was a whole new territory.

When one moves to new places, they are fraught with new scenarios, new experiences, and new possibilities. When Greg failed to do a class work assignment, too interested in his new social gains, I again checked in with Dad, this time letting him know that I'd seen tremendous growth socially and that not completing a class work assignment wasn't all bad. Greg had been distracted by friends, and we could work on the academics. The fact is, we discussed, Greg didn't know how to be the person that he was growing into. Greg's dad liked his new friends, though he worried where his little boy had gone, a bit taken aback by his son's new look and attitude. Greg's dad was encouraged that Greg wasn't obsessing about his failures as much, and he'd taken up guitar. I share Greg's story because teens are constantly having to invent and reinvent themselves, moving from one terrain to the next. When watching *Inside Out*, these conversations become easy to facilitate by using the materials provided.

CASEL's Social Emotional Learning Competencies

CASEL's five Social Emotional Learning Competencies are going to overlap throughout this book, so I'm going to take the opportunity to explain them a bit here. These Learning Competencies provide an entry point for educators to approach social emotional learning on the individual level through *Self-Awareness* and *Self-Management*, then to externalization to *Relationship Skills* and *Social Awareness*, to finally result in *Responsible Decision-Making*. This analysis of how the components work together is simply mine. Others begin looking at the wheel from a different starting point, which is really the beauty of the tool.

As you read each chapter and prepare to teach the unit, know that I'll provide entry points for SEL through the Competencies, but don't limit yourself to the Competency that I zero in on, as most have a way of overlapping. For example, when students complete the pre-viewing activity for *Inside Out*, they are naming their emotions and categorizing them.

This is most easily discussed by thinking about Self-Awareness. It can also springboard into a conversation about Self-Management, as the truly difficult part about emotions is how we actually handle them all!

This particular Pre-Viewing Guide is designed to help students give name to the waves of emotions that they experience every day. In the *New York Times* article "The Importance of Naming Your Emotions" by Tony Schwartz, he writes:

> Emotions are just a form of energy, forever seeking expression. Paradoxically, sharing what we're feeling in simple terms helps us to better contain and manage even the most difficult emotions. By naming them out loud, we are effectively taking responsibility for them, making it less likely that they will spill out at the expense of others over the course of a day.

For many students, this acknowledgment and naming can help curb some of the "drama" of school when teens simply own up to their emotions versus being overtaken by them.

Inside Out focuses on a handful of emotions, but that is more of a movie convention than a psychological reality, and that's okay. That's where, as the teacher, you can walk students through the emotions they name and help them categorize them as well. Depending on how much time you have, the pre-viewing activity could be extended into conversations about the categories of emotions, as that is a topic the movie addresses as well.

As you watch, have students take notes on their note-taking sheet. This note-taking sheet is divided into sketchnote boxes. Students are encouraged to sketch each character and fill the character boxes with quotes or "catch phrases" for each. This will help students follow the movie, but it will also help extend their thinking regarding the emotions themselves. They will use their note-taking sheet to help them participate in the guided discussion once you have completed viewing the movie.

I've recently instituted sketchnotes into my classroom as a way to engage students while working to extend their stamina (see three examples in Figures 1.1, 1.2, and1.3). I noticed that they were not able to sustain silent reading for very long, and I wanted to help them regain this skill that most of my eighth graders, pre-pandemic, typically had. We watched several sketchnoting videos, practiced different ways to organize their notes, and learned some very basic icons. My students really liked Claudine Delfin's video "Sketcho Frenzy: The Basics of Visual Notetaking." I learned a lot myself from the Verbal to Visual channel, hosted by Doug Neil. My "artsy" students loved this, of course, but I was able to help those who were

1. echoed   favorite person.

))))))))

28.
Special!
Plate also
Special!

2. She was famous

4. 10% of people needed medical care.

19. school for the blind. laura went there.

16. Fits = Seziuers

3. She was a delicate   Blind

Plant

7.
me = Enemy

26. Soon enough, she could knit, braid, iron churn and bake all doing this with only touch

her eye Like lava laura erupted...

7 Raised on a Farm

17. as quick as a bunny

18. howe: "tall man"

6. brightest child.

25. Laura couldn't tell bad from good

rsh methods were
ed to get rid of
esses.

20. Laura's story was put in the paper

10. laura was deaf or and blind

laura

8. Dark

24. She's furious

14. Last word =

ause laura was blind and deaf she used touch.

23. laura 's intellictual

rlet fever = her 4 and 7 year olds sisters deaths.

hing to do = house work   1st Page!

22. laura got hurt a lot not knowing what was bad

Figure 1.1

Figure 1.2

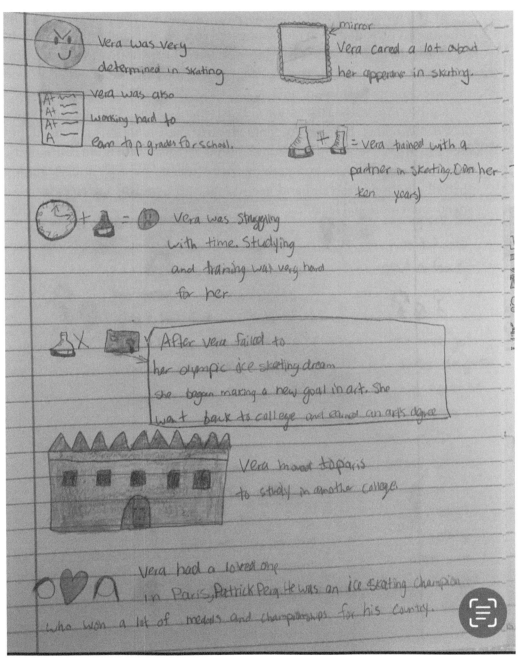

Figure 1.3

self-conscious by explaining that it wasn't really about art, but more about using symbols for efficiency. I have long been a visual note taker, but via different colored pens, highlighters, thought bubbles, stars, underlining, using bullet points, and the like. Once students grasped that it wasn't an entirely artistic proposition, even the reluctant saw the value.

As you watch with your students, pause as you see appropriate, using the timestamps provided. Don't feel obligated to stop and chat unless you want to. This is the goal of these materials: you have the flexibility to use this unit for a week, two weeks, or three or four if you were to use all materials and the assessments in the appendixes.

For this movie, the Discussion Guide is focused on CASEL's Competency of *Self-Awareness*. Helping students identify their emotions is crucial, but doing so in a circle, around the topics posed here, can help build community. Demystifying emotions and making sure students have an understanding that all emotions are valid and useful makes this movie a perfect intro to social and emotional learning.

Name: _____ Date: _____.

Pre-Viewing Guide for *Inside Out*

Trailer:

Watch the trailer to *Inside Out*. In the space below, write a two-sentence summary of what you can determine the movie is going to be about:

_____

_____

_____

Teaser:

How many categories of emotions do you think there are? According to the website verywellmind.com, there are six basic types: happiness, sadness, fear, disgust, anger, and surprise. However, a now famous study published in *Proceedings of National Academy of Sciences* identified 27 different categories. How many can you identify?

Task:

In the space below, draw a tree. The trunk of the tree should represent the whole of your emotions. For every branch you draw, that should be labeled with a major emotion. Then, draw leaves on the branch to represent connected emotions. For example, you could draw a branch that is labeled "happy," and the leaves could be joy, excitement, contentment, etc. There aren't wrong answers, as this is YOUR visualization of emotions. Color your tree to represent connected emotions.

Name: _____ Date: _____

Teacher Stop and Chat for *Inside Out*

TOPIC:	TIMESTAMP:	CHAT:
Headquarters	00:02:56	What emotions do you think you have in your headquarters?
Core memories	00:04:56	What is one of the earliest memories you would like to share?
Solace	00:12:13	Riley seeks solace by activating past positive core memories. How can we learn from this? What memory is a "go to" for you?
Expressing emotions	00:15:03	*"Crying helps me slow down and obsess over the weight of life's problems."* How is this true? Doesn't expressing emotions help us? What stops us from expressing them?
Expectations	00:17:46	*"You've stayed our happy girl."* How can it be hard when people expect us to be happy during difficult times?
Nostalgia	00:23:30	Why do you think sometimes happy memories feel sad?
Islands of Personality	00:26:06	What are your Islands of Personality? How can being overwhelmed lead to a "shut down"?
Abstract thought and Imagination Land	00:42:04	The brain is really complex. Does any of this make you nervous? Does it make things less scary to understand how it works?
Reality distortion lens	00:54:11	This scene shows how our mind can distort reality in dreams. Can this happen while you are awake?

Name: _____ Date: _____

Teacher Stop and Chat for *Inside Out (continued)*

TOPIC:	TIMESTAMP:	CHAT:
Train of Thought	1:00:00	Fear is running through all the things that happened in the dream, essentially a "train of thought." Earlier, Sadness said that the Train of Thought was dangerous. What happens when your train of thought starts to be negative? What can you do to interrupt it?
Joy and Sadness go together	1:02:00 and 1:09:00	Joy and Sadness both like the same memory, but from their own viewpoint. How do Joy and Sadness work in real life? How can these emotions go together?
Bing Bong and imagination	1:11:00	When there is no other way out of the pit, Bing Bong and Joy use imagination to solve their problems. How can you do the same?
Emotions work together to do what is best for Riley.	1:19:00	*"Sadness. Joy needs you."* How can we harness the power of all of our emotions to do what is best for us?
The islands are more complex, and Riley is happier	1:24:00	*"Say what you want, but I think they're all beautiful."* As Riley matures, and as she gets closer to puberty, her emotions are completely connected, but as the movie ends, it asks, *"What could happen?"* How will puberty disrupt the emotions again?

Name: _____ Date: _____

Student Notes for *Inside Out*

As you view the movie, sketch the characters OR a symbol for each character. Use bullet points, thought bubbles, icons, color, size, and highlighting to make your sketchnotes both fun and helpful for you later. You'll be using these notes to have a guided conversation after the movie. Include in your notes:

- an image or symbol,
- catch phrases or quotes the character says, and
- important plot points.

Riley	Joy	Fear
Disgust	**Sadness**	**Dad**
Mom	**Bing Bong**	**Jangles**

Name: _____ Date: _____

Discussion Guide for *Inside Out*

Randomize students, making sure that there is a true mix of students in each group. Create groups of three or five. You'll want an odd number. Have students decide if the following statements are true or false. After they've discussed in small groups, bring everyone back together as a whole and pose the questions. This method of previewing the questions and trying out answers in a small group is a form of rehearsal that helps reluctant students gain confidence to participate.

True or False

It is better to avoid all stressful situations.

Taking risks will lead to happiness.

Moving is always awful.

We should try to hide our embarrassing emotions.

Bottling up your emotions is always wrong.

Nostalgia is amazing. I love to talk about old times.

Sadness and Joy can't really work together.

Anger is always a negative emotion.

You have no control over your Train of Thought.

Notes

Cherry, Kendra. "Emotions and Types of Emotional Responses." *Verywell Mind*, 25 Feb. 2022, https://www.verywellmind.com/what-are-emotions-2795178.

Cowen AS, Keltner D. Self-report captures 27 distinct categories of emotion bridged by continuous gradients. Proc Natl Acad Sci U S A. 2017 Sep 19;114(38):E7900-E7909. doi: 10.1073/pnas.1702247114. Epub 2017 Sep 5. PMID: 28874542; PMCID: PMC5617253.

Schwartz, Tony. "The Importance of Naming Your Emotions." *The New York Times*, 3 Apr. 2015, https://www.nytimes.com/2015/04/04/business/dealbook/the-importance-of-naming-your-emotions.html.

CHAPTER 2

Encanto

Directors: Jared Bush and Byron Howard

Bush:
Zootopia
Moana
Penn Zero: Part-Time Hero

Howard:
Zootopia and *Zootopia 2*
Bolt
Tangled and *Tangled Ever After*
Frozen 2

Easter Eggs:
— "The Family Madrigal" might seem familiar. It was inspired by Belle from *Beauty and the Beast* introducing her town.
— Mirabel's skirt has small details that show her attention to her family members, like a candle for Abuela, flowers for Isabela, and a chameleon for Camilo.
— Butterflies are everywhere in the movie, representing transformation.
— Mirabel's green glasses link her to Bruno.
— Bruno grows a plant in a shoe, just like WALL-E did.
— When Bruno sings "let it go," you can hear the opening notes of *Frozen*'s "Let It Go."

Music: Germaine Franco and Lin-Manuel Miranda

Franco:
Coco
Dora and the Lost City of Gold
The Book of Life

Lin-Manuel Miranda:
In the Heights
Hamilton
Moana

Characters:
Mirabel: Stephanie Beatriz
Abuela: Maria Cecilia Botero
Bruno: John Leguizamo
Felix: Mauro Castillo
Luisa: Jessica Darrow
Julieta: Angie Cepeda
Pepa: Carolina Gaitan
Isabela: Diane Guerrero
Agustin: Wilmer Valderrama

DOI: 10.4324/9781003301790-2

I'm not the kind of person who can watch a movie over and over again; however, *Encanto* has found its way to being played "in the background" as I write this book. What's different? The music. Every single song is somehow both universal and personal. As it turns out, it isn't just me who is obsessing over it. The movie was released on Disney+ on December 24, 2021, and by January 8, 2022, it was #7 on the charts. "We Don't Talk About Bruno" debuted on the *Billboard Hot 100* at #50. "Surface Pressure" reached #54 as well. These two songs encapsulate why I chose *Encanto* for this book. They both are about family dynamics and acceptance, and both relate to CASEL's Competency of *Relationship Skills*. The movie is a study in family dynamics, relationship skills, and the tricky juxtaposition of fitting in and standing out.

Growing up, rivalry doesn't seem like a strong enough word to describe the emotional turmoil between my younger sister and myself. Let's just say if we were Disney characters, she'd be Pocahontas and I'd be Winnie the Pooh. I'm exaggerating a little, but that is certainly how I felt. If you were to ask her, she'd tell you that no one ever noticed her since my "big brain" cast such a shadow. Truth be told, we are both pretty and we are both smart in our own way, but throughout our lives everyone compared us —our parents, our teachers, our coaches, and even our friends. Our situation was not unique, of course, which is why when Mirabel thinks she has to hug her sister to save the family miracle, she's rightfully irritated, and I found myself completely commiserating, along with many others who have lived the comparison nightmare.

One of the ways I introduce a new novel or unit is to find quotes, print them out in different fonts, and tape them to my classroom door. I purposely give them no context, and I don't mention it. There's a ton of great quotes from this movie that would intrigue students:

"In our darkest moment, we were given a miracle."
"Sometimes family weirdos get a bad rap."
"Even in our darkest moments, there's light where you least expect it."
"I'll never be good enough for you, will I?"
"You're the real gift, kid."
"Nothing could ever be broken that we can't fix together."

I put the quotes up a few weeks before we began the unit. Then, on the day we begin, I post each quote to Google Classroom as a question for students to discuss by framing it as an Agree/Disagree. Then, I ask students to respond to each quote and to each other in a digital chat. Once everyone has participated, I talk to students about what I notice from their comments. This is a great way to get all students into the conversation, since they are not being forced to talk in front of the group. I've loved to watch students blossom using this method. Once students feel that their opinions and ideas are valid and supported, they often come out of their shell.

Another approach to introducing this unit would be to use a single quote to begin a discussion of an overarching theme. I'd choose C.S. Lewis's "Comparison is the thief of joy." Today's teens have the entire world to compare themselves to, and the pressures are absolutely palpable. While I wanted a certain brand of jeans because Stephanie in my homeroom wore them, and she was cool, kiddos today face an entirely different brand of pressure. I only had to think about Stephanie and her jeans while at school, but today's teens do not have a respite from pressure; rather, their entire lives are a constant comparison. When people ask how to incorporate SEL into the classroom without changing their entire curriculum, I always remind teachers how much inherent choice we have in where we shine the spotlight. For example, as a 48-year-old mom, I find Abuela's dilemma of how to keep the foundation of her house from crumbling beneath her as she manages multiple generations to be a really interesting question to consider. It is a universal theme, and one that I could choose to explore with students; however, that isn't relatable. "Comparison is the thief of joy," though, will elicit deep engagement from students because I'm choosing to shine the spotlight on a topic that is near and dear to them.

When talking to my Canisius College students who will one day be teachers, I call this the "cell phone" trick. Every teen I know has a very intense relationship with their phone. If you want them to stick with you, use their cell phone in your question. If you want them to think about rights and responsibilities in social studies, ask them to create a contract of rights and responsibilities for cell phone use. If you want them to work out velocity, have them weigh their cell phone and work out problems with their cell phone flying off the roof of a car. If you want to teach persuasion, they can use pathos, logos, and ethos to convince their parents they need a new cell phone. The adults may be sick of talking about cell phone usage, but the kiddos aren't.

When beginning this unit, the Pre-Viewing Guide uses Luisa's song, "Surface Pressure." I chose this song because I know that this is a topic that will appeal to students. While the movie is also about immigration, family, generational aspiration, and a variety of other master's thesis–worthy topics, the one that teens will relate to the most is the one that is most accessible to them. I think there's something sadly profound in the line: "Under the surface, I hide my nerves, and it worsens, I'm worried something's going to hurt us." This is the exact sentiment that I keep hearing from students—the pandemic has left them with a constant fear of what comes next, and waiting to see if everything will be okay or not. Giving students the opportunity to vocalize their anxiety and fears will help them process the trauma they are living through.

The Student Notes section allows me to guide their thinking to topics I want to touch upon, such as symbolism, Abuela's sacrifice and loss, and the metaphor of the enchanted house. It's okay to lead them down the path, of course, but I know that they won't go on the full journey through the unit with me unless I convince them that the trip is worth taking in the first place, which is why I always start with their interests first, and then navigate toward my goals for them. The Teacher Stop and Chat guide allows further discussion around topics that are meaningful, but might need an adult guiding the way. Finally, this particular Discussion Guide places the bulk of the conversation directly with students. These are not small topics, and you can expect students to find many connections to their own lives. Encourage those conversations, even if you feel awkward about them. There is a rawness that can emerge that some teachers want to shy away from, but it is so important to meet these students where they are and help them move through their experiences.

Recently, I had students complete a "Playlist of My Life" where they had to create a slideshow of favorite songs and write a paragraph for each song. My academic purpose was for students to continue to refine their paragraphing skills and practice using commas with coordinating conjunctions. My SEL purpose was to learn more about students and give them an opportunity to share with our learning community after a holiday break and reconnect. I was not prepared for the level of honesty and vulnerability that my students brought to the assignment, but I was amazed by the support that students gave each other. It has become clear to me over the last few years that students are much more willing to participate in community—to be active and caring members—than most adults are, and we must make room for the awkward—allow the awkward space within our teaching—especially when we are teaching those who are at their most awkward. This movie might bring forth some conversations about family and family dynamics that we aren't always comfortable with; however, allowing students space to make connections, see that they are not alone, and process their experiences is both worthwhile in a community of learners and can also be life-altering for those who need a safe space.

Name: _____ Date: _____

Pre-Viewing Guide for *Encanto*

Trailer:

You are going to watch and listen to a song from one of the characters in the story. As you watch and listen to Luisa's song, jot down ten words that you notice or things that occur to you:

1.   2.

3.   4.

5.   6.

7.   8.

9.   10.

Teaser:

We are starting with this song because it captures the underlying theme, or message, of the movie. Look at the words you listed and share them with your group. What did you notice? Dr. Valerie Long, a clinical psychologist who specializes in pediatric psychiatry, writes in "Teens Stress Is Higher than Ever": "The message teens receive about overachieving is contributing to the rise in unhappy, overstressed, anxious and depressed adolescents and young adults." Does your group agree?

Task:

With your group, write a summary statement about Luisa's feelings about her gift. As you watch the movie, you'll be noting how characters feel about their gifts.

Write your statement here:

_____

_____

_____

Name: _____ Date: _____

Teacher Stop and Chat for *Encanto*

TOPIC:	TIMESTAMP:	CHAT:
Mirabel's gift	00:09:02	Do you ever feel like everyone you know or your whole family has a gift, but you don't?
Family picture	00:22:16	Mirabel is left out of the picture. Did they do this on purpose? Or did Mirabel not include herself? Do you ever feel like this with family or friends?
"I'm not fine."	00:23:00	Do you ever struggle to express when you are "not fine"? Why? Don't we all feel like that sometimes?
The house is in danger	00:26:40	How does it feel when people don't believe your version of things?
Abuela knows about the cracks	00:29:55	What could the cracks represent?
Luisa, "the strong one"	00:34:21	Luisa is defined by her single trait of being strong. Do you ever feel that being strong (physically and/ or emotionally) is too much for teens?
We don't talk about Bruno	00:45:45	What could Bruno represent? He lives among the family, but he is ignored, and no one ever talks about him. How does this impact everyone?

Name: _____ Date: _____

Teacher Stop and Chat for *Encanto (continued)*

TOPIC:	TIMESTAMP:	CHAT:
Bruno	00:57:10	Bruno says that his gift wasn't helping his family, but he loves his family, and even stays nearby but out of sight. How does this make you feel?
Butterfly	01:03:00	Have you noticed butterflies in the movie so far? Now they are going to lead Mirabel to the solution to the problem with the magic.
Cactus flower	01:08:00	Isabela admits that she was only marrying for the family. When she does this, she creates a unique cactus flower. What message do you think this is giving us?
"You suffered so much . . ."	01:22:00	We realize that Abuela has suffered so much for her family. What sacrifices have your friends and family made for you?
"Look at this home. We need a new foundation."	01:25:00	What lesson do you think this song has for us? What foundation could multiple generations create?
"What do you see?"	01:29:00	Where is the real magic?

Name: _____ Date: _____

Student Notes for *Encanto*

Your teacher will pause for you to answer the following questions as you watch *Encanto*. The theme that we are going to notice is this: *Everyone faces pressures, and we can help each other through hard times.* Our relationships will improve when we practice good communication and seek to understand each other.

Question:	Answer:
Everyone talks about Mirabel's lack of a gift. What are your thoughts about this? From what you can tell so far, what might Mirabel's gift be?	
We learn that Abuela knows about the cracks. Why do you think she keeps this information secret from the family? Is this a good or bad thing?	
Bruno is a forbidden topic. Is this a healthy approach? What might the family do instead? Could this be a part of the "crack in the foundation" of the house?	
Butterflies symbolize transformation. Who or what do you think needs transforming? Where are some of the places you notice butterflies?	
When Mirabel really hears Abuela's story of the miracle, she realizes that part of the miracle involved great suffering and sacrifice. How is this different than what we think of when we hear the word "miracle"?	
"Look at this home. We need a new foundation." What does that mean to you? Explain what this means literally (the physical foundation) and metaphorically.	
What do you think will change as they rebuild the house and community? How will the theme be addressed this time?	

Name: _____ Date: _____

Discussion Guide for *Encanto*

Create a circle so that students can all see each other. Students are going to participate in a Rotating Chair Discussion. This discussion requires that students both talk *and* listen. The teacher will pose the question, then call on Student A. Student A will answer, and then they will look around the circle for another student whose hand is raised to participate. Student A will then call on Student B. Student B (and all others who participate after the first comment) will need to begin with one of the following statements:

- I agree with Student A, and I think . . .
- I agree with Student A, but I'd also add . . .
- I disagree with Student A because . . .
- I can see Student A's point; however, . . .

The teacher should post these sentence starters on the board and remind students to begin this way. Students will then be able to share their thoughts, call on the next student, and so on. When the teacher thinks the question has been fully answered, the teacher can summarize. For advanced conversations, a student can be assigned as a moderator.

Rotating Chair Questions:

1. This movie focuses a great deal on the expectations of "making your family proud." Is this a reasonable expectation or no? Explain your answer.
2. The house is "alive" in this movie. In what ways does the director do this? Is this a good metaphor? How are houses "alive"?
3. Gender stereotypes are challenged in this movie. Give examples and explain how the director challenges the stereotype. What do you think the director was trying to make us understand?
4. The concept of perfection and beauty is also challenged. In what ways do you see that happen? Think about the cactus that is created instead of a rose in the scene with Mirabel and Isabela. What does that mean?
5. Abuela, for most of the movie, is quite rigid. She doesn't want to change or stray from her own thinking. How does that change at the end of the movie?

Note

Long, Valerie. "Teens' Stress Is Higher than Ever." *Children's Resource Group—A Multi-Specialty Behavioral Health Practice*, 27 Oct. 2019, https://www.childrensresourcegroup.com/crg-newsletter/stress-anxiety/teens-stress-higher-ever/.

CHAPTER 3

Soul

Director: Pete Docter
Inside Out
Up!
Monsters, Inc.

Easter Eggs:
— In the Hall of Everything, there is:
  • A Pizza Planet truck
  • A whale from *Finding Nemo*
  • Luxo the Lamp
  • A streetcar from *Coco*
  • Sprites from *Princess Dream World Castle*
— When walking past a store, Joe sees a sign selling "9 Inch Nails," which is a nod to Trent Reznor, who is the lead singer of the band with that name AND one of the composers for the music in this movie.

Music: Trent Reznor and Atticus Ross
The Social Network
The Girl With the Dragon Tattoo

Characters:
Joe Gardner: Jamie Foxx
Terry: Rachel House
22: Tina Fey
Paul: Daveed Diggs
Dorothea Williams: Angela Bassett
Moonwind: Graham Norton

DOI: 10.4324/9781003301790-3

I watched *Soul* three times before I decided to include it in this book. It's not that I didn't like it, or immediately notice all the ways it connected with SEL. Rather, it was the amorphous message that troubled me. I couldn't really put my finger on the theme, and it left me with a little bit of an existential crisis the first two times I watched. It pointedly asks the question, "What's the meaning of life?" And frankly, I wasn't feeling sure I could tackle this with students. Then, my husband and son started watching it one evening. I wasn't paying much attention, having already watched it twice. I was scrolling on my phone, both watching and not, as you do, when Joe's former middle school student calls him up to tell him about a gig. That's when it came rushing at me: a grown man calls his middle school band teacher to hook him up with a gig. *Put another way: Joe had such an impact on his students that they remembered him when they were adults.* He influenced the lives of children, instilling in them a love of music, a passion that some continued to pursue for their whole lives. *That* is the meaning of life, at least for me as a teacher and a mom: inspiring others to be their best selves, pursuing the passions I help them discover.

Once I decided to include it, I started researching. What I found is so interesting in itself, so worthy of sharing with students, that the movie is almost secondary. Pete Docter, when he and his team at Pixar decided to create Joe as Pixar's first Black lead character, recognized that he was going to need help. According to Insider.com's article, " 'Soul' codirector admits he was 'afraid' to talk about race before working on Pixar's first movie with a Black lead," Docter said, "I am because I'm afraid I'm going to stick my foot in my mouth and say something dumb and offend somebody. I did along the way, without knowing it, and I learned from other people's mistakes as well." Kirsten Acura, the article's author, goes on to explain, "They also created an internal brain trust made up of Black Pixar story animators and artists to make sure the film accurately reflected Black culture." THIS. This is the message that we need students to understand: it is okay to recognize your limitations and lack of knowledge when it comes to other people's culture and experience, and the most respectful, socially responsible way to approach this is through asking them to teach you.

This is easier for younger students to do because they have fewer preconceived notions, and they are less shy about asking blatant questions. When I was growing up in Newport News, Virginia, in the 1980s, racial tensions were high. My district participated in a controversial bussing experiment, which resulted in me being one of only a handful of White kiddos who lived close enough to the elementary building to stay there, while most of my White, suburban neighbors were bussed to the downtown elementary school. The Black kiddos came to Jenkins Elementary School in my 99% White neighborhood. The result of this bussing situation has had a huge impact on my interests and experiences, because, even though I lived in a White suburb, I went to school where the vast majority of the students were Black. I am fascinated that the first biography I ever read was of Harriet Tubman. That W.E.B. Dubois was a part of my elementary curriculum. *Representation matters*. Through my entire elementary experience, I was a minority, and it has given me a different lens than I would have had otherwise. So many of the convictions I hold are because I had the experience of "other" at such a young age.

My best friend was a little girl named La'Vonda Love Bell (which I thought was the best name ever invented). When I started this chapter, I decided to see if I could find her on Facebook. I reached out, and we were able to connect! We reminisced a bit, and agreed that it was pretty remarkable that we had a special friendship, despite the tensions that existed in the world around us. I did have an "outsider" experience in elementary school, and much of it wasn't very good. However, La'Vonda and I were able to ask each other questions about the others' world, and I am so thankful that this relationship defined "race relations" for me. La'Vonda and I are 48 years old, so this is ancient history—we were in the same kindergarten class, so this anecdote is 43 years old, but it really puts things in perspective for me when I consider that Pixar has created its first Black lead. *Representation matters*.

Of CASEL's Social and Emotional Learning Competencies, *Social Awareness* is the trickiest in our current political climate. CASEL describes Social Awareness as "The ability to understand the perspectives of others and empathize with them, including those from diverse backgrounds and cultures." *Soul* is the perfect movie to help students with this concept in a non-threatening way. Joe, the protagonist, is a middle-aged, Black middle school teacher. No matter who the kiddos are in my room, they aren't going to have that much in common with Joe, at least on the surface. This allows me space to explore the universality of all our experiences. The Pre-Viewing Guide asks students to think about all the wonders of living. The notetaking sheet helps focus students' attention on Joe's influence, helping to guide them toward the post-viewing discussion. The Discussion Guide helps students think about how all the things that make life worth living—our relationships and our passions all help us lead a meaningful life.

Name: _____ Date: _____

Pre-Viewing Guide for *Soul*

Trailer:
Watch the trailer for the movie *Soul*.

Teaser:
Joe, the protagonist, dies on what he thinks is the best day of his life. One of the key considerations of this movie is determining what makes life so magical. In other words, what simple pleasures make life worth living? Create a list below. Consider your five senses, your experiences, and memories. For example, hot apple cider on a fall day or the feeling of sliding into home plate. List ten things:

1.   2.
3.   4.
5.   6.
7.   8.
9.   10.

Task:
With your group, take turns sharing the items on your list. Together, create a statement about the types of things that make life worth living. Try to make the statement accurate for everyone, so really drill down to the nature of what we all find valuable about life. Write your statement below, and be prepared to share both your list and your statement:

_____
_____
_____

Name: _____ Date: _____

Teacher Stop and Chat for *Soul*

TOPIC:	TIMESTAMP:	CHAT:
"Hang on, hang on. What are y'all laughing at? So Connie got a little lost in it."	01:47:00	Is there something that you do that you "get a little lost in"?
"I would die a happy man if I could perform with Dorothea Williams."	04:55:00	Notice the foreshadowing here. We know from previews that even though Joe dies, this is a movie about how he lives.
As Joe gets carried away by the music, the background fades into colors and becomes ephemeral	07:48:00	Follow this artistic decision in the movie. When we are dealing with the "soul" in any way, the edges soften, creating a dreamy quality.
"Is this where personalities come from?"	00:15:39	This is the Great Before. This theory suggests that people are born with certain traits. Do you have any traits that you think you were just born with? Any talents?
Hall of Everything	00:19:24	If you are a Pixar fan, the Hall of Everything contains dozens of Easter Eggs. Look for: a Pizza Planet truck, a whale from *Finding Nemo*, Luxo the Lamp, a streetcar from *Coco*, *Princess Dream World Castle*, and more.
"My life was meaningless."	00:24:44	Joe was a great teacher and musician. Why might he think this?
"You can't crush a soul here. That's what life on Earth is for."	00:26:36	What are some things that happen on Earth that can be "soul crushing"? Do people have a choice if something crushes them, or is it out of their control?

Name: _____ Date: _____

Teacher Stop and Chat for *Soul (continued)*

TOPIC:	TIMESTAMP:	CHAT:
"You know, lost souls aren't that different from those in the zone. The zone is enjoyable, but when that joy becomes an obsession, one becomes disconnected from life."	00:33:53	Have you ever known anyone who has become obsessed with something so much that it lost its joy? Maybe obsessed with winning or achieving?
22, in Joe's body, learns about taste	00:41:37	What are your favorite tastes? Is there anything you eat that you always take the time to savor?
Sticking with things we love isn't always easy	00:48:31	Connie gets ridiculed for her talent. Why would someone do that? How can we handle a situation like Connie's?
"Talk about having a spark. This guy was born to be a barber."	00:51:43	What makes Dez born to be a barber? Does it matter that Dez didn't get to be a veterinarian? Why or why not?
Joe finds out that you aren't assigned a purpose or meaning of life	01:12:00	How do you find your purpose? The meaning of life?
Dorothea explains the parable of the fish	01:16:00	What does this parable mean?
Joe studies the artifacts of his day, collected by 22	01:18:00	What lessons does Joe figure out from the artifacts of his day?
"I'm not good enough. And I never got my spark."	01:26:00	How can negative comments make us feel like we aren't good enough? How can we combat that type of thinking?
Joe gets a second chance at living, and when Jerry asks how he's going to spend it, he says, "I don't know, but I am going to live every minute of it"	01:30:00	What do you think Joe will do with his second chance? What does it mean to live every minute of our lives?

Name: _____ Date: _____

Student Notes for *Soul*: Joe's Lessons

As you view the movie, take note of Joe's lessons. When you find an example of the lesson listed, jot it down. Keep a tally of how often you notice the lesson.

Don't judge a book by its cover.	Don't take the joys of life for granted.	Don't get into a negativity spiral.
Goals are good, but they shouldn't define you.	Always look for ways to help others.	Don't underestimate your influence.
Never give up.	It's all right to slow down.	Look for connections.

Name: _____ Date: _____

Discussion Guide for *Soul*

Prepare for the Discussion

Soul's ending leaves viewers wondering what happens to Joe. This allows the viewer to speculate what they think Joe does with his second chance. There are really four options:

A. He takes the full-time teaching position.
B. He declines the full-time teaching position, and he plays with Dorothea.
C. He does a combination of both.
D. He decides to look for other paths to follow with his second chance.

Which do you think Joe does? Use your "Joe's Lessons" note sheet to help you predict what he might do. With your small group, choose one of the above options and provide as many reasons as you can to support this idea.

Think With Your Feet

Label each corner of your classroom with letters A through D, as indicated above. Then, have students who think Joe takes the full-time teaching position go to corner A. If they think he declines, have them go to the B corner. If they think it is a little of both, have them go to corner C. Finally, if they think Joe is going to explore brand-new options, have them go to corner D.

In each corner, have students use sticky notes to list their reasons for their belief about Joe's future. After students have exhausted their ideas, have students rotate to another corner. There, they should study the reasons. Have them continue to rotate and study the reasons provided by their peers.

Finally, after students have looked at evidence in all four corners, have them "think with their feet" again. Would they all go back to the same corner they had started in originally, or were they swayed by the evidence to change their mind? End this activity by debriefing what they've learned about Joe and what may have influenced their final discussion.

Note

Acuna, Kirsten. "'Soul' Codirector Admits He Was 'Afraid' to Talk about Race before Working on Pixar's First Movie with a Black Lead." *Insider*, 7 Jan. 2021, https://www.insider.com/soul-movie-black-criticism-pete-docter-2021-1.

CHAPTER 4

The Mitchells vs. The Machines

Director: Mike Rihanna **(feature directorial debut)**
Gravity Falls (voice actor, creative director, and writer for Season 1 and creative consultant for Season 2)

Easter Eggs:
— *Dial 'B' for Burger* is Katie's way of paying homage to Alfred Hitchcock's film *Dial 'M' for Murder*.
— The new PAL headquarters resembles the aesthetic of the 1982 cult classic *Tron*, which is about a computer programmer who is sucked into his software.
— Globe of Colorado is a reference to Mall of America, one of the largest malls in the world.

Music: Mark Mothersbaugh (lead singer of the new wave band Devo, whose song "Whip It" remains a cult classic)
Rugrats
Muzak for Insomniaks

Characters:
Katie Mitchell: Abbi Jacobson
Aaron Mitchell: Mike Rianda
Linda Mitchell: Maya Rudolph
Rick Mitchell: Danny McBride
PAL: Olivia Colman
Mark Bowman: Eric Andre

DOI: 10.4324/9781003301790-4

I watched *The Mitchells vs. The Machines* with my daughter, Zoey, who is currently a junior in high school. We visited her dream college just last week, and she has started talking her future into existence. Zoey's hopes and dreams about her future are starting to be the main topic of conversation, and I am teary when I think of her going to college. Don't get me wrong, I am wildly excited for her. My college years were some of the best of my life, a time when I truly discovered who I was, but I'm going to miss my best friend. I know it is an unpopular opinion, but I value our friendship over all else, and I always have. She and I have gone on Target runs since she was born, bonding over our shared love of planners, bags, and shoes. Zoey has a servant's heart, and her greatest dreams are to be a language teacher (she's double majoring in French and Spanish) and a missionary. Somewhere along the way she plans to find a husband who wants to travel, make her coffee, and have adventures with her own kids, whom she plans to raise bilingually and in backpacks traipsing across the world.

As much as I adore Zoey, she has one strange characteristic: she is not impacted by emotional movies. As a family who watches *a lot* of movies, we all find this somewhat disturbing. We've often asked, "Were you watching the same movie as us?" We have a family story we always pull out about her stoic attitude about movies. When the kids were little—too little to watch this for sure—we watched *The Help*. I'm guessing that Zoey was around ten and Oliver was seven. When the movie ended, Oliver and I were pretty much ugly crying. Zoey, on the other hand, stood up, and asked what was for dinner. Oliver and I were so appalled that we still tease her about this. I tell this story to explain what I loved about *The Mitchells vs. The Machines*: It made Zoey, my stoic, cry! I couldn't believe it when I heard the tell-tale sniffles. I said, "Zoey Rain Chandler. Are you crying? Over a movie?!" She said, quite accurately, "Mom, it just isn't subtle at all. Like, THIS is what it feels like to be a teenager."

Zoey is referring to the protagonist, Katie, and I find this fascinating. Zoey is nothing like Katie, who is an artist, a loner, listens to loud music, and is, quite unremarkably in the movie, not heterosexual. I was puzzled that my daughter was so moved, like moved-to-tears moved, by this movie, given that the protagonist is not relatable to her in any obvious way I could see. I asked Zoey to explain more about this, and she couldn't really put her finger on it except to say that Katie's desire to "find her people" and Katie's excitement over getting to use her talents in college were so familiar. The other reason she was crying, she said, was that the family was finally accurate to what "real families" are like.

Full disclosure—my family, like the one in the movie—is a bit on the quirky side, so I can see the resemblance that made her teary. My husband, like Mr. Mitchell, believes that the world would be a better place if social media in any form would simply disappear. My son, though not autistic like Aaron, the little brother, has had one "obsession" after another. He developed a British accent from Thomas the Tank Engine, so much so that at his kindergarten screening, they asked if his father was British. Later, he wrote extensive fan fiction when he was obsessed with *Star Wars*. More recently, he got a Rubik's cube for his birthday in April and had gotten the "solve" (to use cyber lingo) down to "sub one," which means under a minute. Mrs. Mitchell is constantly smoothing things over within her family, but will go absolute Mama Bear if anyone messes with her family. The mom is also the most neurotypical in a family whose quirks are very noticeable. She may or may not seem a bit like me when she overexplains the family members to each other to keep the peace.

As you may have gleaned from this chapter so far, this movie is really different from others you may have watched with your own kiddos. It is a sci-fi, animated, man vs. the machine conflict, where the family happens to have an autistic son, an openly queer daughter, and they are tasked with saving the universe. While this all sounds very chaotic, that is the absolute beauty of the movie. It isn't chaotic because it isn't about any of those individual topics. It isn't about autism. It isn't about homosexuality. It isn't about dysfunctional families. Instead, it is an action-packed adventure that is fun, engaging, and emotional in all the right ways. It is the story of a family. A real, authentic, quirky family. There are no villains, no dead parent tropes, no dark sibling rivalry. Those stories exist, and they have their place, but it was refreshing to watch a movie that could seemingly have a heavy political agenda simply tell a story and let the viewers draw their own conclusions about what makes this family tick.

With that being said, there are some districts where this movie would ruffle more than a few feathers, and thus I'd suggest proceeding with caution. However, I've arranged the materials in a way that allows viewing without prolonged conversations about the more controversial issues. (As an aside, I personally don't find neurodiversity and homosexuality to be controversial, but rather factual, but I've lived the last several years with a heightened awareness of those who do.) The Pre-Viewing Guide, Stop and Chat questions, and the Student Notes do not zero in on these topics. However, the Discussion Guide is another story.

The Discussion Guide is the dream scenario—it is for those of you who have the autonomy and freedom to do what should be done. It allows conversations to happen that would broaden students' respect for each other, deepen understanding, and open up lines of communication that would change the community of your classroom. Would I show this movie? It depends on the year and the collection of families involved. This year, I have 100% of the permission slips returned, families that have been supportive, and no one has questioned what I teach. However, last year, I had families who took offense that I was teaching Amanda Gorman's "The Hill We Climbed" inauguration speech in my English class. I was raked over the coals on Facebook for teaching *The Pigman*. No, I would not have shown this movie last year because it would have landed me on the news.

This is where your professional judgment comes in. The best way, I find, to approach this situation is to truly know my students' families. I always send a survey out to families, and I include spaces for them to tell me what I need to know. Given the political upheaval of last year, you wouldn't be surprised to learn that I would choose not to watch this movie then. However, I applaud those who would still fight these battles, who might have a huge amount of support from their district, or who simply believe what they believe and are willing to do the work that so desperately needs to be done to change the future.

The SEL connections are clear in this movie, particularly as it relates to the neurodiversity issue. Aaron, Katie's ten-year-old brother, though it is never stated, is likely on the autism spectrum. He exhibits many characteristics of autism: stimming, difficulty with communication and eye contact, repetitive actions, deep interest in a single subject, and literal thinking. Yet, the movie doesn't put those characteristics under the microscope; rather, it is simply a part of who Aaron is. He's sweet, funny, devoted to Katie, and a willing conspirator in her movies. He's brave, and he loves his family. Making sure that students who view the movie recognize his contribution to the family and allowing space for conversations about his neurodiversity goes a long way towards addressing CASEL's Competency around *Social Awareness*. Students very likely already know another student with some of these same autistic qualities, and how we showcase Aaron is crucial to our society's greater acceptance of those who are not neurotypical.

Additionally, as was true with *Soul*, representation matters. The powerful message we send to students who may be on the autism spectrum when we show a movie like this—a movie that isn't about the differences but about the commonalities—is much needed. As I said, this movie will make some people uncomfortable, but I chose to include it for that very reason. Some people are ready and able to take those kinds of risks in the classroom that could very well change lives.

As for the issue of Katie's sexuality, the movie provides an off ramp for those who might not be willing (or able) to discuss this in class. The movie has a sort of false ending once the Mitchells have saved the world. Enough, in fact, for me to believe the movie was getting ready to go into an ending montage. I had rounded the corner into the kitchen when Zoey called me back to tell me there was more. In the segment that is labeled "Six Months Later," there's the line that brings all of the innuendo into the light of day. On a FaceTime call, Katie's mom asks if her and Jade are "official" and if she is going to bring her home for Thanksgiving. There had been hints throughout the movie: an LGBTQ+ flag pin, as well as some Easter Eggs that related to queer filmmakers, but overall, the movie isn't about Katie being gay. The movie is about a teenage girl who wants to "find her people" and follow her passion for filmmaking. This is why it is so relatable. Much like Aaron, the director doesn't make the movie about differences, but rather about how much all teenagers are ready to leave home, get away from their lovable but overbearing families, and get their lives started.

If nothing else, I hope that this movie guide could be used to specifically support students who are neurodivergent or queer. Please note that I am using the word "queer" with guidance from my go-to resource, *Learning For Justice's* "Best Practices for Serving LGBTQ Students":

We recognize the complicated history of the word queer and that its reclamation as a positive or even neutral term of identity isn't universally accepted. In this guide, we use queer as an inclusive term to refer to those who fall outside of cisgender or heterosexual identities—not as a pejorative.

If you are worried that the students in your classroom are unfamiliar with neurodiversity or homosexuality, you could be right, but I doubt it. The fact is, my son, Oliver, who is in eighth grade, only uses they/them pronouns with students he knows prefer it. Unlike some adults, this isn't difficult for him, and it isn't awkward. It is simply how a growing number of students are identifying. As with most things, our students are very often ahead of us in their ability to accept and handle the nuanced truths that are found in our schools.

Name: _____ Date: _____

Pre-Viewing Guide for *The Mitchells vs. The Machines*

We will be watching a movie with the central conflict of Man vs. Machine.
Before we begin, discuss these statements with your partner. Decide if you
agree, disagree, or aren't sure. Fill in the chart below together.

Statement	Explain What It Means	Agree, Disagree, or Unsure (explain your thinking)
Technology has made us less human and separates us from each other.		
Technology can be used for great good or great evil. People are the deciding factor.		
Technology allows artists, musicians, and creative works to come to life and for people to feel connected.		

Name: _____ Date: _____

Teacher Stop and Chat for *The Mitchells vs. The Machines*

TOPIC:	TIMESTAMP:	CHAT:
"I've always felt a little different than everyone else. So I did what any outsider would do: made weird art."	02:43:00	Do any of you find comfort in creating or making art?
Katie says it didn't bother her when her dad didn't share her interest, yet there's a broken heart on the screen, and her body language says otherwise	05:07:00	Why might Katie deny that she's sad or that it hurt her feelings that her dad didn't share her interest?
"After all these years, I'm finally going to meet my people."	06:00:00	Katie has been 100% uniquely herself, even though she didn't have many people supporting her. Isn't that pretty difficult, though?
"The Poseys are on vacation right now, and look how happy they are."	00:16:40	First, consider the name Poseys. (Poser, posing—in other words, not real.) How can social media make things look better than they actually are?
"I am experiencing this. This is how I experience things."	00:25:33	Katie is trying to relay to her dad that her phone/technology/digital world IS her world. Do you feel that way? If so, do others understand this? If not, do you understand Katie's perspective?
"Watch what happens when I turn off the Wi-Fi."	00:35:08	Everyone in the movie proceeds to lose their minds without Wi-Fi. This might be dramatic, but how does it feel when you aren't connected? Is this okay or something to worry about?
"We have a chance to save the world, and we are going to do it."	00:44:38	Now that Katie is reminding her dad what kind of person he really is, what do we learn about Katie's true opinion of her dad?

Name: _____ Date: _____

Teacher Stop and Chat for *The Mitchells vs. The Machines (continued)*

TOPIC:	TIMESTAMP:	CHAT:
"Are you now my mother?"	00:58:02	In the middle of this apocalyptic scene, Katie's mom refuses to leave the "robo-boy" behind. What does this say about her relationship to a robot? What message might that have for us?
Katie finds out from watching the video on the recorder that her dad sacrificed for her	01:15:19	How do parents and families sacrifice for their kids? Why is this difficult for kids to see and understand?
Katie's dad is horribly incapable of figuring out how to get YouTube onto all the screens	01:22:19	How might someone unfamiliar with computers feel when they hear and see others navigating so easily?
"You changed your programming. Is that possible?"	01:25:31	Katie's dad is using a computer, against what we might have believed to be possible. What does this suggest to us about people who fear technology?
"If this obstinate man could change his programming, we decided we could change ours. We make our own orders now."	01:28:27	Even though this is a touching moment in the movie, what might the director be suggesting about AI (artificial intelligence)? Should we be concerned?
"I like it. It looks like us."	01:33:03	The picture that is on the front of the magazine isn't "ideal," but Katie's mom knows it is who they are. What kind of family do you want to have in the future?

Name: _____ Date: _____

Student Notes for *The Mitchells vs. The Machines*

Since Katie's animation style frequently uses "thought bubbles," your notes will, too. As you view the movie, we'll be stopping to chat. Fill in the thought bubbles with your ideas! This will be helpful later when we have our final discussion after the movie.

Name: _____ Date: _____

Discussion Guide for *The Mitchells vs. The Machines*

We are going to be doing a discussion about each of the four Mitchells. We'll be reading each statement that critics have said about the character, and then let our conversation grow from that statement. We'll call on each other in a Rotating Chair format.

1. Reuben Baron, in his article for CBR.com, "*The Mitchells vs. The Machines* Breaks New Ground for LGBTQ Representation in Animation," writes: "*The Mitchells vs. The Machines* does an amazing job centering a queer hero. It doesn't make her queerness the focus of the story but also makes it explicit in a way that can't be ignored." **Why is this an important statement about Katie's characterization?**

2. According to " 'The Mitchells vs. the Machines' Celebrates the Beauty of Neurodivergence," by Jodie Hare, "Aaron struggles to socialize with people outside of their family," and "Aaron struggles to have a conversation with a neighbor he likes, leading him to repeatedly stutter and speak in a scream-like tone" while also being deeply interested in dinosaurs. **How do Aaron's special interests and specific traits as a neurodivergent kiddo help save the world?**

3. According to Optimistjenna.com, Mr. Mitchell "struggles with social imagination. This means guessing how others would react to his behavior." Mr. Mitchell himself says, "We don't think like normal people." **Even though Mr. Mitchell and Katie struggled to connect, how does that situation change? What does that tell us about relationships?**

4. Linda Mitchell, the mom, has a "somewhat insecure side that stems from her jealousy of her neighbors, the Poseys, who display the image of a 'Perfect Family.'" **At the end of the movie, when an imperfect picture of the Mitchell family ends up on the cover of a magazine, Linda says, "I like it. It looks like us." How does their epic road trip change Linda?**

Notes

Baron, Reuben. "*The Mitchells vs. The Machines* Breaks New Ground for LGBTQ Representation in Animation." *CBR.com*, 5 Sept. 2021, www.cbr.com/mitchells-vs-machines-katie-lgbt-animation/#:~:text=The%20Machines%20Breaks%20New%20Ground%20for%20LGBTQ%20Representation%20in%20Animation,-By%20Reuben%20Baron&text=Tweet%20Share%20Email-,The%20Mitchells%20vs.,main%20character%2C%20is%20openly%20LGBT.

"Cory Collins and Jey Ehrenhalt. Best Practices for Serving LGBTQ Students." *Learning for Justice*, 29 Jun. 2022, https://www.learningforjustice.org/magazine/publications/best-practices-for-serving-lgbtq-students.

Hare, Jodie. " 'The Mitchells vs. the Machines' Celebrates the Beauty of Neurodivergence." *Bitch Media*, 1 Jun. 2021, www.bitchmedia.org/article/the-mitchells-vs-the-machines-neurodivergence-celebration-review.

"Linda Mitchell." *Sony Pictures Animation Wiki*. https://sonypicturesanimation.fandom.com/wiki/Linda_Mitchell.

Mitchell, Jenna. "The Mitchells vs. The Machines and Autism." *Optimist Jenna*, www.optimistjenna.com/mitchells-vs-machines-autism/

CHAPTER 5

Wreck-It Ralph

Director: Rich Moore (directorial debut)
Later co-directed *Zootopia* and *Ralph Breaks the Internet*, the sequel (he is also a voice actor)

Easter Eggs:
— The high score on the main screen of Fix-It Felix, Jr., 120501, refers to the birthdate of Walt Disney, December 5, 1901.
— Oreos guard the King's castle, and their chant of "O-re-o" is a reference to the guards at the palace in *The Wizard of Oz*
— There are nearly a hundred video game references throughout, including characters from Sega, Nintendo, Capcom USA, Namco Bandai Games, and many more.

Music: Henry Jackman
Kong Skull Island
Winnie the Pooh
Big Hero Six
Puss in Boots

Characters:
Wreck-It Ralph: John C. Reilly
Fix-It Felix: Jack McBrayer
Vanellope von Schweetz: Sarah Silverman
Sergeant Calhoun: Jane Lynch
King Candy: Alan Tudyk

DOI: 10.4324/9781003301790-5

I'm going to date myself here, as a woman of 48, but I'll try to paint a picture for those of you never lucky enough to spend a Saturday afternoon in an arcade with a sweaty fist full of quarters. First of all, there was bound to be some requisite rule that it had to be dimly lit. As you walked in from the brightness of the mall, it was a bit like walking into a cave. The music was loud, but not loud enough to drown out the sounds of Pac-Man, Ms. Pac-Man, Centipede, Gallaga, Frogger, Qbert, and Donkey Kong. Just to make sure you are experiencing this as you should, "Billie Jean," "Girls Just Wanna Have Fun," and of course "I Love Rock and Roll" were piped in, there was a couple in a dark corner making out—hands in each other's back pockets—and the air was thick with cigarette smoke. For me, this was the early 80s, and by today's parenting codes, it seems unfathomable, but let me tell you, my Conservative (with a capital C) Christian, overprotective parents handed me a $5.00 bill and returned two hours later. There was nothing, and I mean nothing, as exciting as adding your quarter to the line of them on the crevice of glass of the game you were waiting to play, waiting your turn, listening to music, and simply disappearing into another space for a few hours where all that mattered was putting your initials in for achieving a high score.

Wreck-It Ralph is amazing because it can evoke those memories in me while at the same time appealing to today's students. The arcade isn't nearly as seedy in the movie as it was in my reality, but the nod to us older folks is there. That's not why I chose to include this movie, but it is an added bonus. The reason this movie was on the list from day one is that my family has watched it a hundred times. We are two adults, a boy and a girl three years apart, and we all love it. That is not easy to achieve—it hits right for adults, multiple-aged children, and across gender. There are very few movies that meet that criteria for us, so this was a natural pick. However, the real reason we've watched it so many times is that Oliver, my now middle schooler, would always settle in to watch it. He was not a settle-in kind of kiddo, to put it mildly.

This morning I decided I'd go to my true audience, middle school kiddos, and asked Oliver what his thoughts were, and he said:

It's a movie about connections and outcasts. Both Ralph and the Glitch Girl—I forget her name—are outcasts and the movie shows that you don't have to be like everyone else to have friends. You wait and find the right people for you. It's unlikely, you know? Wreck-It Ralph and some Candy Crush-ish character. But it works.

I asked him what he thought about the fact that when Vanellope (Glitch Girl) is able to be healed of her "glitching," she doesn't want it written out of her code. He said, "Yeah, I mean, you shouldn't have to change who you are. She's a Glitch Girl and staying that way is who she is. Her code is her DNA." Oliver knows what kinds of books I write, and he's always been a good sounding board, but this was particularly interesting to me given that he is currently in middle school. As he grabbed his bowl of mac and cheese and headed to his room, he looked over his shoulder and said, "So, that's my hot take on the complex world of middle school, mom." He was mocking me, to be sure, but it showed me, yet again, just how much a middle school student can glean from a movie, and reinvigorated me to dig deep into the Social and Emotional implications of the movie.

I'll speak first to what he says, and then add a layer that he may not have noticed. That's the nature of using movies in a classroom. The Pre-Viewing Guides are as much for the teacher to take the temperature of students' background knowledge, emotions, and thoughts around the topic the movie takes on as it is to ignite the students' interest. The need for connection is important to all of us, but in *Wreck-It Ralph*, there is a layer of loneliness and "otherness" that I often see in the classroom. Oliver isn't wrong to suggest that the movie is about outcasts, for sure, and that is what the focus is for the Pre-Viewing Guide. The Teacher Stop and Chat will help pull students' attention toward the "deeper" layer that is also there: the socioeconomic disparities that can cause students to experience rejection.

There are two scenes that encapsulate this "deeper" dive into the movie. The first is early on when Ralph is lamenting that he lives on a trash heap. You can't get much more obvious, so this is a really good conversation point to focus students' attention on how the socioeconomic situation is impacting the storyline. Ralph literally lives in the shadow of Fix-It Felix's opulent home. Ralph is narrating, so we get to hear it straight from him:

> Felix and the Nicelanders go hang out in their homes . . . which he's just fixed and everyone, you know. . . . They go to their homes, I go to mine, which just so happens to be . . . a dump. And when I say a dump, I don't mean, like, a shabby place. I mean, an actual dump, where the garbage goes . . . and a bunch of bricks and . . . smashed building parts; that's . . . that's what I call home.

Students will easily understand who the "Nicelanders" are, and how Ralph feels about it.

The second example is when Vanellope is trying to construct her race car. According to the Disney Fandom Wiki:

> It was made out of scrap materials she found at the local junkyard and ran on pedal power. It consists of matcha swiss roll as the front body, a wafer as its main body, a marshmallow as a seat rest, various cookies and chocolate dipped pretzels as the wheels, and a white flag.

While this may seem cute and harmless, when her car is compared to all the other racers, it is clear that hers is made from scrap; Vanellope lives in Diet Cola Mountain, further separating her from her peers. The socioeconomic landscape of the movie is an excellent entrance point to help students think about SEL concepts.

For example, conversations can be directed to discuss the unexpected friendship between Ralph and Vanellope and focus on CASEL's Competency of *Relationship Skills.* Or, for more mature and older audiences, the discussion can be directed towards CASEL's Competency of *Social Awareness.* Either way, this movie is an excellent choice to approach the trope of the "outcast" and dissect the reasons that this "otherness" may happen, and the ways we can, as a community, combat this very typical problem students face in schools.

I grew up in a solidly upper middle class home, and I don't think I ever thought about socioeconomics until I met my husband when I was in graduate school. He and I, to put it mildly, were from different worlds. His story isn't that different from many of my students now: single mom, not nearly enough money for all the mouths to feed, second-hand clothes, bad haircuts, and a troubled school life. He'd worked since he was 14, not to save for a trip to Paris, as our own daughter is doing, but to get the free meals from working in a diner, and to help his mom keep the lights on. Our lives were about as different as one can imagine, and the opportunities present in my everyday life were never available to him. Join a club to make sure colleges could see how well-rounded I was? Impossible. He went to work. Get a tutor, like I did, when I was failing statistics? Impossible. His mom would have to work three hours to pay for one half hour of the help I received. Play high school sports? He could never have afforded the shoes and clothes necessary to do so. The list goes on and on, but it is safe to say that we could have sat in the same high school classroom, and I never would have known him as a person, nor him me. I'd have seen a withdrawn kid who guarded his heart with a smart mouth and quick retorts. He'd have only seen a privileged girl whose problems included having to stop and buy gas for her car that morning, making her late to homeroom, while his mom walked two miles to work each way in all kinds of weather.

One of the roles I take seriously as a public school teacher is to make sure that students understand that their destinies aren't fixed to their family's experiences in life. Unfortunately, there are not nearly enough adults helping students see that their potential lives can be different, especially in cases of generational poverty. Additionally, I share with my students that the life I led as a teen, with a new car for my 16th birthday, country clubs, and exotic vacations, did not follow me into adulthood. I chose a different path, one that involved doing a job that I love and marrying someone who did not even have a bank account when I met him, much less any money in it, but was the best conversationalist I'd ever met and had a heart of gold. I share this with students to make sure that they understand that yes, their starting points are impacted by the socioeconomic situation they are born into, but they do have paths and choices that will forever impact their futures.

Middle school may seem early to begin this type of conversation, but I've found that students already understand many facts about the world that they've been forced to deal with. I'll never forget a young woman in my eighth grade class, sharing with me that her mom had lost her license because of a DUI, and she was going to have to drop out of band because it was mandatory to perform in the concerts to pass. My heart broke, of course, but luckily, I was able to help her work out a ride from a friend. She'd thought of this before, but was deeply ashamed of the reason she'd need a ride. We rehearsed some ways to handle the situation until we found a way to get through it without revealing her mom's story.

It isn't just those experiencing poverty who are often facing the harsh adult world head on. I had another student whose parents had left him and his 17-year-old brother home alone while they went to a destination wedding for a week. He missed school for two days in a row because he'd never gotten himself up for school before. His parents somehow thought these two boys would be okay, but as it turned out, both kiddos were really nervous at night, even though their home had a security system. I emailed back and forth with the 17-year-old and reassured him that the noises he described were not unusual, but convinced him to call his aunt to come stay with them for the last few nights. From the outside, everyone would have said these two boys had it all, but they would have been wrong.

I share these examples because both stories illustrate important truths about teens. First, they are often handling "adult" issues, things that one would hope wouldn't be a consideration for them for many years. Second, students should not assume that the grass is always greener on the other side.

Often, I hear students who have socioeconomic stability wish they didn't have the intense pressure to have perfect grades, be good at sports, and even find the perfect dates for dances. Then, I hear other students who would love the opportunities that those with socioeconomic stability have dismiss their wealthier counterparts' problems. It is crucial for communities—both in our classroom and in our neighborhoods—to understand that we all have problems, we all have choices, and we are all on paths that we didn't choose. The goal of my class, in many ways, is to help students realize that there are other paths, and at the heart of it, we make decisions that either move us closer to the goals we have for ourselves or further away. We aren't relocated to our single "lane" for life, and much like Wreck-It Ralph and Vanellope, we don't have to be ashamed of where we came from in order to end up creating a different story.

Name: _____ Date: _____

Pre-Viewing Guide for *Wreck-It Ralph*

Our pre-viewing activity for *Wreck-It Ralph* is a free-write that you'll then share with a partner. In the movie, the protagonists both have "sore spots" that impact their actions and happiness.

Task One

When we know that someone will respond badly about a topic, we sometimes say, that's a "sore spot." It's a great description, right? If you press on the topic, it will hurt. In other words, it is a "touchy" subject. Think about a sore spot you have.

Choose a "sore spot" that you would be willing to share with a partner. (Example—you hate being picked last for teams in gym, or you are a horrible artist and hate when people tease you.) Talk this over with your partner. After you have both shared, work with your partner to answer the following question in the space provided.

Task Two

Question: What are some things we can do if a person has a "sore spot" and we discover it? How can we make things easier for them? What could someone do to make your "sore spot" less noticeable?

_____

_____

_____

_____

_____

_____

Name: _____ Date: _____

Teacher Stop and Chat for *Wreck-It Ralph*

TOPIC:	TIMESTAMP:	CHAT:
Exclusion	03:09:00 and 00:12:49	Ralph is excluded from events and lives on a trash heap. Why might he be excluded? How does it feel to be left out?
"Labels not make you happy. Good! Bad! You must love you."	05:19:00	What are some of the labels that you hear? Are all labels bad?
"Game's busted."	00:22:00	When Ralph doesn't show up to work, the game doesn't function—it's busted. What does this tell us about Ralph's role in his community?
"It's not her fault. She's programmed with the most tragic backstory ever."	00:32:00	Sergeant Calhoun's "tragic backstory" makes her act in certain ways. However, do we have to keep behaving in certain ways because of our past? Pay attention to this character's story arc.
"Listen! This event is pay-to-play. We all know this. The fee to compete is one gold coin from your previous winnings, if you've ever won."	00:34:03	In order to compete, an avatar has to have a coin, which they'd have to have won previously. In this scenario, who gets to even be in the race? Is this similar to anything in the real world?
Vanellope first "glitches" when she is in anxiety-producing situations; some have said that this is ADHD or Tourette's	00:35:45	What can happen to people when they are anxious? What physical responses can we notice? When you are having a physical reaction to anxiety, how would you like people to respond?
The gang of girls break Vanellope's car and mock her glitching	00:41:58	This is clearly the worst kind of bullying. Why would anyone do this? Why does it bother Ralph so much?

Name: _____ Date: _____

Teacher Stop and Chat for *Wreck-It Ralph (continued)*

TOPIC:	TIMESTAMP:	CHAT:
Ralph: "I tried to warn you kid, I can't make things. I just break things." *Vanellope: "I love it. I love it."*	00:51:18	Ralph was worried that his creation was bad, but Vanellope loved it. Do you ever find that you are hard on yourself when other people aren't?
"Glitches can't leave their games. It's one of the joys of being me."	00:55:57	Vanellope explains how she is limited by her glitch. How does our society handle limitations? How should we?
Vanellope uses her glitch to escape from King Candy	01:21:41	What do you think this suggests about Vanellope's "disability"? Consider that it is her self-acceptance that saves her.
"Fix-It, get behind me."	01:23:42	Traditional gender roles are reversed here as Calhoun takes the lead in protecting Felix. How does this impact your view of Fix-It? Calhoun?
"There's no one I'd rather be, than me."	01:25:40	Ralph has found satisfaction in being himself because Vanellope sees him as a hero. How do other people's positive opinions of us help us to accept ourselves?
"I'm thinking more along the lines of a constitutional democracy. President Vanellope von Schweetz."	01:29:42	What statement is Vanellope making by refusing to be the princess, and instead becoming the president?
"And the players love her, just like I knew they would. Glitch and all. Turns out I don't need a medal to tell me I'm a good guy, because if that little kid likes me, how bad can I be?"	01:32:01	What does Ralph's final statement tell us about our need for friendships and community?

Name: _____ Date: _____

Student Notes for *Wreck-It Ralph*

One of the ways that we learn about characters is by analyzing what they look like, what they say, what they do, what they think, and what others say about them. Choose to focus on one of the following characters: Wreck-It Ralph, Fix-It Felix, or Vanellope von Schweetz, and complete the chart:

Character:

What they look like:	What they say:	What they do:	What they think:	What others say:

*Students can be directed to discuss their character with someone who picked the other two characters or compare and contrast with someone who chose the same character.

Name: _____ Date: _____

Discussion Guide for *Wreck-It Ralph*

Post the following quotes in a slideshow or on the board. Ask students to use "fist to five" to rate how much they either agree or disagree with the quote. (Fist equals 0 and means strongly disagree, and 5 is fully agree.)

Then, have students take turns explaining their rating and how it relates to the movie. Ask students which character it applies to the most.

"Crowded hallways are the loneliest places, for outcasts, and rebels, or anyone who just dares to be different." —Hunter Hayes	"Take very little notice on those who choose to treat you poorly. It is how they are defining their story, not yours." —Lei Wah	"The hardest thing about being an outcast isn't the love you don't receive. It's the love that you long to give that nobody wants." —Jodie Blanco
"You are the author of your own life. . . . Don't let others define it for you. Real power comes by doing what you are meant to be doing, and doing it well." —Oprah Winfrey	"Poverty is like punishment for a crime you didn't commit." —Eli Khamarov	"I decided that the most subversive, revolutionary thing I could do was to show up for my life and not be ashamed." —Anne Lamott
"The only thing that will make you happy is being happy with who you are." —Goldie Hawn	"Loneliness and the feeling of being unwanted is the most terrible poverty." —Mother Teresa	"We sometimes think we want to disappear, but all we really want is to be found." —Unknown

Notes

Ansello, Edward. "The Most Terrible Poverty." *Scholars Compass*, Virginia Commonwealth University, https://scholarscompass.vcu.edu/cgi/viewcontent.cgi?article=1016&context=vcoa_editorial.

Brainy Quote. www.google.com/search?q=The%2Bonly%2Bthing%2Bthat%2Bwill%2Bmake%2Byou%2Bhappy%2Bis%2Bbeing%2Bhappy%2Bwith%2Bwho%2Byou%2Bare.%E2%80%9D&rlz=1C9BKJA_enUS986US986&oq=The%2Bonly%2Bthing%2Bthat%2Bwill%2Bmake%2Byou%2Bhappy%2Bis%2Bbeing%2Bhappy%2Bwith%2Bwho%2Byou%2Bare.%E2%80%9D&aqs=chrome.69i57j0i30l2.6600j0j4&hl=en-US&sourceid=chrome-mobile&ie=UTF-8.

"Invisible Lyrics by Hunter Hayes, 4 Meanings. Invisible Explained, Official 2022 Song Lyrics." *LyricsMode.com*, 27 Jan. 2014, www.lyricsmode.com/lyrics/h/hunter_hayes/invisible.html.

Jd, et al. "Great Quotes by Oprah Winfrey That Will Empower You." *Sources of Insight*, https://sourcesofinsight.com/oprah-winfrey-quotes/.

"A Quote from Please Stop Laughing at Me . . . One Woman's Inspirational Story." *Goodreads*, www.goodreads.com/quotes/339632-the-hardest-thing-about-being-an-outcast-isn-t-the-love#:~:text=%E2%80%9CThe%20hardest%20thing%20about%20being%20an%20outcast%20isn't%20the,t%20have%20many%20choices%20available.

"Sometimes You Think You Want to Disappear but All You Really Want Is to Be Found." *Brian Weiner*, 24 Dec. 2021, https://brianweiner.com/sometimes-you-think-you-want-to-disappear-but-all-you-really-want-is-to-be-found/.

Stanford Center on Poverty and Inequity. *Inequality.com*, https://inequality.stanford.edu/publications/quote/eli-khamarov#:~:text=Quote%3A,crime%20you%20didn't%20commit.

Svoboda, Martin. "So Rita and I Decided That the Most Subversive, . . ." *Quotepark.com*, https://quotepark.com/quotes/1463268-anne-lamott-so-rita-and-i-decided-that-the-most-subversive-re/.

"'Take Very Little Notice on Those Who Choose to Treat You Poorly. It Is How They Are Defining Their Story, Not Yours.': Poor, Treat Yourself, Story." *Pinterest*, 25 Mar. 2015, www.pinterest.com/pin/take-very-little-notice-on-those-who-choose-to-treat-you-poorly-it-is-how-they-are-defining-their-story-not-yours-58406126394058906/.

"Wreck-It Ralph (Character)." *Disney Wiki*, https://disney.fandom.com/wiki/Wreck-It_Ralph_(character).

CHAPTER 6

Lemonade Mouth

Director: Patricia Riggen (adapted from Mark Peter Hughes's book)
Under the Same Moon
Girl in Progress
Miracles From Heaven
TV series episodes for *Jack Ryan*

Easter Eggs:
— The band members all start the movie wearing orange or purple, except for Mo. She wears blue like her boyfriend, but as the band gets together, she wears orange and purple, too.
— Principal Brenigan says he used to be a "rebel," which is a hint towards his role as a T-bird in *Grease 2*.
— The author has a cameo in a bee costume at the Halloween Bash.

Music: Bridgit Mendler (and other members of the film cast).
Wizards of Waverly Place
Good Luck Charlie

Characters:
Olivia White: Bridgit Mendler
Wen Gifford: Adam Hicks
Mo Banjaree: Naomi Scott
Stella Yamada: Hayley Kiyoko
Charlie Delgado: Blake Michael

DOI: 10.4324/9781003301790-6

Much like I grew up on after-school specials, teens today have fond memories of made-for-TV movies from Nick Jr., the Cartoon Network, PBS Kids, and of course, Disney. Many of the musical artists students listen to today got their start by starring in these movies, and the appeal seems to cross all demographics of students. I've never heard more students agree on anything than when I bring up their early viewing habits. The fact is, before they were old enough to find their niche corners of the internet, parents like me parked their kiddos in front of the television while we were making dinner or folding laundry, or in my case, writing books and grading papers. Teens have a collective experience that comes from the way we, a generation of parents who grew up glued to television sets, introduced kiddos to movies.

I didn't really understand how powerful this group dynamic was until recently when my co-teacher and I were discussing an assignment we'd designed called "Playlist of My Life." They were asked to choose five songs, video games, television shows, or other media to create a "playlist" of their lives so far. We used this to reconnect with students after a break and to hone their paragraphing skills since they had to explain their choices. Over and over, the song "Life is a Highway" was on our students' lists. It was the most popular song from the Disney/Pixar hit movie *Cars* in 2006. My co-teacher and I were confused, since they were too young for this to be their favorite movie. However, when we dug a little deeper, we found that this was the song they'd grown up with because they all had older siblings who were obsessed with the movie when they were just babies. That song was literally some of the first media that they remember and love because they were exposed to it so early. It would be a mistake to ignore the pull that music has on our students.

Lemonade Mouth is the perfect example of a character-driven music story that appeals to a wide variety of students because, by design, Disney has included "types" that pretty accurately reflect the mix of students one would find in today's high schools, even though this movie was released in 2011. My own kiddos have been commenting on their memories of watching this over and over, and we've all been impressed that the movie has aged well. This idea of "aging well" makes choosing which movies to include overwhelming.

Many movies that I loved are dated in a way that would be hard to explain. I showed my own kiddos *Goonies*, and they thought it was both weird and cruel. I adored *Sixteen Candles*, and it is plainly homophobic and racist, while handling sexual assault carelessly. My daughter went through a *Grease* phase when she was little because I thoughtlessly played it for her. Wow. I was mortified when she was singing along. However, *Lemonade*

Mouth, I think, will stand up to the test of time because it is charming and consciously brings these "types" together in a *Breakfast Club*-esque way, in detention, but avoids the tropes that are now making me cringe. As this book moves from animated films to live action movies, I'm struggling to make sure that the choices are relatable for a classroom of students. Frankly, there's just something about animated movies that seems to appeal to everyone. Live action films are a bit trickier.

Why then, if I'm worried about appealing to a classroom of students, might I start with a movie that has a soundtrack of pop songs that go with it? I was a little worried that the music might be off putting, but it isn't because it is honest and fits the storyline: a group of students stuck in detention, all of whom are very different "types," begin to tap, snap, stomp, clap, and play the instruments that are now in the basement, since the principal is solely focused on the sports teams. What they find is that they are a nice mix who can create a unique sound while expressing themselves. You have to suspend your disbelief, as it is highly unlikely spontaneous music will erupt from strangers in detention. But, that's the charm of this movie—you are willing to suspend your disbelief because it is a storyline that you really wish would happen. You are even willing to pretend that their sound is unique, when it is really very catchy pop music!

The appeal, as I've mentioned, is in the ability for students to find at least some aspect of at least one character relatable. There's actually quite a bit of depth to their characterization, which could be explored separately. Here's a rundown of the characters:

Olivia White:

- Lives with her grandmother because her mom left and her dad is in prison for some "bad decisions" he made since her mom left. For most of the movie she doesn't even speak with her dad.
- She's lonely and humiliated by her family.
- Her best friends are her grandma and sickly cat.
- She has serious stage fright and performs best when she's spontaneously moved to sing the songs she is writing in private.

Wendel "Wen" Gifford:

- Slight lisp when he speaks.
- Mortified by his father's choice of a 28-year-old girlfriend.
- Really wants to be a star—wants to call the band Wen.
- Proves to be a very good friend and has a crush on Olivia.

Mohini "Mo" Banjaree:

- Traditional Indian family with a father whose expectations are unrealistic for an American teenager.
- "I'm classically trained. I don't play whatever *this* is!"
- Her father wants her to constantly seek extra credit and worry about college.

Stella Yamada:

- Passionate and outspoken, she's portrayed as the rebel.
- The "Question Authority" shirt that she gets in trouble for to start the movie really foreshadows her entire personality.
- Greatly encourages others to use their voice to express themselves.
- Desperately wants her family's approval, even though she doesn't act like it.

Charles "Charlie" Delgado:

- Though his parents love him, he's constantly compared to his older, more successful brother.
- There's "sibling rivalry" vibes throughout, though it is driven by the parents' comparisons, not the actual sibling.
- Has a hard time speaking up for himself.

Teenagers and adults alike can take these characters and find at least some attributes that they relate to, making the ensemble cast a good choice for facilitating discussions.

The goal of using this movie is to initiate three conversations. In the Pre-Viewing Guide, students will begin thinking of the dangers of labeling others without knowing their backstory. In the Stop and Chat, the conversations are more pointed, really digging into the dynamics that keep students from building community within school. Finally, in the Discussion Guide, the conversation is going to turn to solutions. Students are asked to create a "perfect school" and will struggle to balance the needs of all students, just like educators do.

Using this movie in your classroom will add a level of novelty that I think is missing in school. We know that students love music. We know that they learn when they are relating to one another. I plan to use this movie as a reward for my middle schoolers at the end of the year. They will be primed for conversations about labels, social dynamics, and the need to be heard, as they make their move to high school. Will my hallmates be a bit surprised that my students are singing along to an old movie from 2011? Probably. But, that's okay. It's most important that my students have moments like this that will shore them up for high school.

Name: _____ Date: _____

Pre-Viewing Guide for *Lemonade Mouth*

Before we watch *Lemonade Mouth*, we are going to do some brainstorming. This movie has an underlying message about the dangers of labels. We all have labels that describe us, but labels often limit us to just those characteristics when we are all so much more.

In the chart, fill in positive associations with each label and negative associations for each label. At the bottom of the chart, answer the questions about labels.

Label:	Positive Association:	Negative Association:
Leader	in charge	bossy
Athlete		
Musically talented		
Smart		
Reader		
Rebel		
Gamer		
Quiet		
Talkative		
Creative		
Artist		

Why do labels make it difficult to truly know a person?

_____

_____

_____

Which labels might fit you? What association do you mostly face for that label?

_____

_____

_____

Name: _____ Date: _____

Teacher Stop and Chat for *Lemonade Mouth*

TOPIC:	TIMESTAMP:	CHAT:
Every person has their own struggles	07:59:00	In the exposition, we are learning that all different kinds of people are dealing with their own struggles. Why do you think this is easy to forget?
Blended families	00:11:28	Wendell is angry about his dad's girlfriend. This is a normal response to a new situation. However, there are lots of different types of family configurations. Let's name those we know.
"No, he actually let me off with a warning. You know, I got soccer practice, some big games coming up."	00:11:46	Sometimes people get special treatment for their social status. How does that feel? Should rules always be applied equally?
It is impossible to measure up to everyone's expectations of you	00:14:08	Delgado doesn't want to play soccer, even though his brother was a superstar. Do you ever experience sibling rivalry? What can we do about it?
Question authority	00:15:59	Stella causes a scene at the assembly. She may have some good points, but what happens when she impulsively disrupts the assembly instead of planning how to address her problems?
"This is the underground."	00:16:55	Robotics club, Shakespeare society, Chess club, ballet, Mathletes, art club, the school newspaper, and AV club have been relegated to the basement. What does that tell us about what the principal values? Do you think this is always true?
"There's a moment where stars align and fates collide, creating that perfect union. This was that moment."	00:18:28	Have you ever found just the right person at the right time? We should always keep our eyes and hearts open to meet people who may be different from us, but who may become very important. How could being judgmental get in the way of this?

Name: _____ Date: _____

Teacher Stop and Chat for *Lemonade Mouth (continued)*

TOPIC:	TIMESTAMP:	CHAT:
"People, they—they need to hear you. . . . You deserve to be heard."	00:22:38	Why would it be so difficult to take the chance to form a band? What do they have to lose? To gain?
"I've never met any of Olivia's friends."	00:44:30	Wen comes to Olivia's house and we find out that she hasn't really had friends over before. Why not? Why is it so hard to make and keep friends? What gets in the way?
"That's Lemonade Mouth. That's our band."	01:21:30	Once the school hears the band at the Halloween Bash, their message really resonates. Why do you think they are suddenly so popular?
"I'm finding my way. But I deserve for you to just let me be me."	01:29:39	When our wishes are different from our families, it is hard to have honest conversations. How do you think the kids in the band are doing with their conversations? Any surprises?
Both bands can be good	01:35:00	When the bands play against each other, there's a sense you have to choose between them. What is wrong with liking both bands? Is it okay to have friends with different opinions or from different groups?
When Lemonade Mouth falls apart on stage, their fans save them	01:37:00	It takes a lot of courage to be the first one to speak up or sing or do anything alone. Explain what this scene is trying to convey to us.
"Sometimes risking it all to have your voice heard pays off in ways you never imagined."	01:41:43	What ideas might you have that need to be voiced? What's stopping you?

Name: _____ Date: _____

Student Notes for *Lemonade Mouth*

As you watch, identify the label that might be applied to each character. Then, find examples of the trait being viewed as positive and times that the trait could be viewed as negative.

Character:	Trait:	Positives:	Negatives:

Name: _____ Date: _____

Discussion Guide for *Lemonade Mouth*

This discussion will take a few class periods. It will be predominately among students, so the teacher should circulate, ask questions, and keep students on task. Students who are shy or don't know each other well will take a bit to get warmed up, but the benefits of peer-to-peer teaching and learning make this worth the awkward moments.

Directions

The class should be divided into five equal groups. Each group will be given a character to focus on. The group is going to use their notes and ideas about the movie to create a "one pager" about the character. Give each group a sheet of plain white paper or poster board, colored pencils or markers, and the following list of requirements:

- Include a symbol to represent the most important thing to the character
- Include five POSITIVE SENTENCES about the character
- Include a quote from the character (students may Google quotes)
- The character's name should be written creatively and large enough to be seen from three feet away.
- Include important relationships, events, and ideas about the character

Once students complete their "one pager," make sure it is colorful and positive. Post their sheets around the room, making sure that no sheet is too close to another.

Provide students with sticky notes to do a gallery walk. In their group of five, have students find a "one pager" to study. Give them three minutes at each station to leave notes for each other. Notes should be compliments about the work, offer an addition, or ask a question.

Debrief the activity and then distribute a second sheet of white paper. Ask students to do the same assignment, but this time for themselves. Let students know that their "one pagers" will be displayed and provide them ample time to complete them.

Closing conversation: after students have created their own "one pagers," ask students how they feel. Does it feel like a risk to be positive about oneself? Why? What can we do as a class community to normalize viewing ourselves in a positive way?

CHAPTER 7

Hidden Figures

Director: Theodore Melfi
St. Vincent
Going in Style

Easter Eggs:
— Two airplane paintings that are in the background when Johnson and Harrison are talking are from the original main headquarters of NASA field center at Langley Airforce Base.
— A woman in a white scarf is meant to represent Cece Bibby, the artist who painted a special design for John Glenn.

Music: Hans Zimmer, Pharrell Williams, and Benjamin Wallfisch
Zimmer:
Interstellar, The Gladiator, Dune, The DaVinci Code, Inception

Williams:
"Happy," "It's On Again," "Freedom"

Wallfisch:
Blade Runner 2049, The Starling, Mortal Kombat, It

Characters:
Katherine: Taraji Henson
Dorothy: Octavia Spencer
Mary: Janelle Monae
Harrison: Kevin Costner
Vivian: Kirsten Dunst
Jim: Mahershala Ali
Mr. Zielinski: Aleksander Krupa

DOI: 10.4324/9781003301790-7

Hidden Figures is immediately recognizable as a movie about segregation and race relations, but there's another layer that really spoke to me. Mary Jackson is a mother, a wife, a Black woman, and an aspiring aeronautical engineer. Her struggles are not only with segregation and sexism, but with the expectations imposed on women as homemakers and mothers. While movies and books about sexism often portray women being kept out of the workplace or hitting a glass ceiling, it isn't often that there's real attention paid to the struggle that so many women still feel today: who are we, at our core, when not simply fulfilling the roles we play in others' lives? In other words, as Mary says, "We go from being our father's daughters, to our husband's wives, to our babies' mothers." That truth bomb got me thinking, and I haven't been able to shake the feeling that there's an important opportunity here.

Of course, I'm feeling this as a mom, wife, daughter, teacher, author, union president, and friend. It seems that the balance between all those roles is precarious at best, and I am usually left wishing for more hours in the day. I usually feel that I am disappointing someone, and quite frankly, I'm sure that it isn't just me feeling that way. It is impossible to pour from an empty cup, as the saying goes. I've written before about how difficult it is to "keep all the balls in the air" in terms of time management. I haven't looked at it through a *Relationship Skills* lens, and that would certainly be an approach to this movie. How do we navigate relationships and responsibilities and still hold on to our own identity?

Without sounding too cynical, I sometimes find myself wondering, who am I if not the sum total of my roles, most of which are in relation to other people? What if all of those roles and responsibilities weren't my biggest priority, and instead *I* was my biggest priority? What if, when I needed rest, I took it? What if, when I was angry, I expressed it? What if, when I needed attention, I demanded it? These may sound like no-brainers—of course I could do those things. Of course I could, until we drill down to the complexities of our roles and relationships. Setting boundaries, developing good self-care routines, and advocating for ourselves are lofty goals, and as I get older, I'm working on this. What, then, could I impart to students using this movie?

During the course of watching and discussing the movie, and interwoven into the questions and comments, I want students to understand that they have innate value—value as human beings without the labels attached. As corny as it sounds, I want students to begin thinking of themselves as enough, just as they are. This is the stuff of inspirational cards and Facebook posts, I know, but the truth is terrifying: students today have more pressure than most of us ever had at their age. I have eighth graders who are obsessed over college, and my daughter has friends who sleep four hours each night because they are so over-involved with a combination of sports, school, working, and trying to maintain their Insta-image. These students have a lot more in common with me than I'd ever really considered until I began thinking about this chapter. We are all stretched too thin, and we need to change the narrative for our students. There is dignity in just being who you are. It is there, no matter if you are high performing or not. It is there if you don't play sports, and it is there if you are quiet and shy. Our dignity—our wholeness and feelings of being "enough" —need to be tied to who we are instead of what we do.

After talking it over with my own teens and gauging what they know about segregation and women's rights, bias based on gender, and the like, I decided this chapter would have to center on those topics, too. My children knew a good deal about these topics, but both agreed that watching a movie like *Hidden Figures* and having a space to talk about those issues was important. My daughter, Zoey, who is 17, actually added a phrase that made the hair on the back of my neck stand up. She said, "especially now." She has watched, just as I have, as our country has become more and more divided; she has watched the course content get a little watered down because teachers do have to have some self-preservation; she has watched as *Saturday Night Live* skits have tapped into the absurdity of overzealous parents who storm school board meetings. I agree, we need to talk about these issues, *especially now.*

With the weight of that comment, *especially now*, I realized that there is a way to approach this topic that ties my questions of identity and self to the racial and gender bias. There is a thread that runs through both of these ideas that I decided to pursue in this chapter, and that commonality is simple: all folks—man, woman, Black, White, young, old, housewife, engineer, mama—deserve dignity.

There are many powerful moments in the movie, but when Katherine, one of the human computers, is forced to run, in heels, a half mile each way to the "colored" ladies' room, it is evident that segregation robs her of her dignity. When she finally cracks, it is because a White man, her boss, mocks her for the time she spends in the bathroom. Her monologue brings me to tears because she suffered in silence, put her head down, and just did what she had to do. It was only after her outburst that those around her really understood what this segregation meant on a base level: the most fundamental of human needs—to go to the bathroom—required a round trip of a mile, in heels, no matter the weather.

My dad's greatest gift to me was to instill this same "just put your head down and do what you have to do" attitude. It's served me well, to be sure, but it is also how boundaries disappear and 50- and 60-hour work weeks are born. So, as I thought about what I wanted to do with this chapter, it became a study in dignity in all we do—both in our own lives and how we help others to live theirs.

In the Pre-Viewing Guide, the goal with students is to activate their prior knowledge around racism and sexism. It is also to signal to students that we aren't going to just watch a movie about Black women—we are going to watch a movie about women who are Black. By this, I mean that I want students to recognize that different situations would cause different levels of bias, and that both are intolerable. The Student Notes page gives students a place to trace the different ways that segregation and sexism happen to all of the female characters. However, the Teacher Stop and Chat isn't only focused on the bias, but on the relationships, especially how they change over time. This movie does a great deal to represent the slow progress both women and Black people made during this time period, but it also shows how minds can be changed. Many of the White male characters, and notably two of the White women characters, come to an understanding—at least a little—about segregation and sexist policies, but it is only through relationships with those who were being hurt. Ideology changes with relationships.

The final Discussion Guide helps students process what they watched, and they work in small groups before sharing with the whole. The one question that is really central to the experience of this movie is "What do you think of when you think of the word 'equality'?" It is my hope that as students have traced the experiences of these three Black, female mathematicians, who contributed so courageously to the space race, that they might recognize the desire we all have for dignity.

Name: _____ Date: _____

Pre-Viewing Guide for *Hidden Figures*

Often, we study the discrimination or bias against a particular group. In the case of *Hidden Figures*, there are two different ways that discrimination occurred: because the mathematicians were female and because they were Black. Try to imagine what it would be like to be a female, Black mathematician working at NASA in the 1960s. If you aren't sure, do a Google search and scan the results. Before we view the movie, using your knowledge from social studies, fill out the chart below with your group and write a summary statement of your discussion. Try to think of at least three ways they might be discriminated against.

Discrimination because they were female	Discrimination because they were Black

Write a summary statement below. Include your findings from both parts of the chart.

_____

_____

_____

Hint: you can begin with "We determined that . . ." or "Our group thinks that . . ."

Name: _____ Date: _____

Teacher Stop and Chat for *Hidden Figures*

TOPIC:	TIMESTAMP:	CHAT:
Computers	00:11:56	Have you ever thought of the fact that the word "computer" first referred to people who do computing? Does this surprise you?
Shoe stuck in the grate	00:13:40	Women wore dresses and heels, even if it wasn't practical. What could the stuck high heel represent? What about taking off the heels to watch the test?
Mary: *"I'm a Negro woman. I'm not going to entertain the impossible."* Mr. Zielinski: *"And I'm a Polish Jew whose parents died in a Nazi prison camp. Now I'm standing beneath a spaceship that's going to carry an astronaut to the stars. I think we can say we are living the impossible."*	00:15:26	This interaction is really important to set the tone for the movie. How are both of their statements true at the same time? Why might Mary not want to think about the engineering program? Why might Mr. Zielinski want to help her?
"Sorry. I have no idea where your bathroom is."	00:21:25	This basic necessity sets up one of the biggest conflicts of the movie. Note that she can't use the women's bathroom, as it isn't marked "colored." How might you imagine this plays out? How would you feel?
"Colored" coffee pot is set up for Katherine, though no one made it for her	00:39:29	Who do you suppose did this? Why?
No one measured to see that the IBM computers would fit through the doors	00:41:07	What does this oversight tell us about NASA's knowledge of what they were doing, and computers in general?
"Give her everything she needs to work on Shepherd's trajectories without redactions."	00:45:27	Katherine is able to figure out what a room full of men can't, even though she has to read through the redacted (darkened out) lines. How do the men feel about this? How do you know?

Name: _____ Date: _____

Teacher Stop and Chat for *Hidden Figures (continued)*

TOPIC:	TIMESTAMP:	CHAT:
"Every time we have a chance to get ahead, they move the finish line."	00:47:12	What does Mary mean by this?
Mary and her boys get kicked out of the White-only library. On the bus she says, *"Separate and equal are two different things. Just 'cause it's the way, doesn't make it right."*	00:50:23	Mary is trying to keep her boys out of trouble when they see the protesters, but then she explains to them that what is happening isn't right. Why might Mary want to keep her boys shielded? Why does she choose to tell them anyway?
The man who sits across from Katherine hands her the telephone for her to call her family and explain the new working situation (working late, no extra pay)	00:56:43	How does this gesture speak volumes about how her role has changed? Compare this with the coffee pot situation. What has changed?
"No more colored restrooms. No more White restrooms."	01:04:06	What prompts Harrison to change the rules about the bathrooms? If he cared about this, why hadn't he done it before?
"We all get to the peak together or we don't get there at all."	01:29:10	What does Harrison mean when he says this? How does this apply to the movie? Society in general?
Mary became NASA's and America's first female African American aeronautical engineer	01:57:34	What obstacles did Mary have to overcome as a female, an African American, and a wife/mom?
Mrs. Vaughn becomes supervisor over White women	01:57:48	What obstacles might she face? Has she proved she can handle it? How?

Name: _____ Date: _____

Student Notes for *Hidden Figures*

As you watch, take notes when you notice discrimination based on either of the two categories we discussed in the Pre-Viewing Guide. Fill out the chart below as you view.

Katherine	Mary	Dorothy
Examples of racial discrimination:	Examples of racial discrimination:	Examples of racial discrimination:

Please note: in many cases the discrimination was because of race *and* gender. You may record those in either category and put a star next to it to indicate both.

Name: _____ Date: _____

Discussion Guide for *Hidden Figures*

As we consider the messages of the movie, let's evaluate how we see discrimination happening around us today. Answer the questions below in preparation for our conversation.

1. Do you think there is still gender discrimination? If yes, provide examples. If not, support your answer as well.
2. Though not in the movie, in what ways can men be discriminated against? (Think about jobs, emotions, biases, etc.)
3. Do you think there is still racial discrimination? If yes, provide examples. If not, support your answer as well.
4. What does the word "equality" make you think of?

Teachers: once students have brainstormed these questions alone, have them pair up with a random partner and discuss. After there's been time to chat in pairs, ask the groups to share their answers to one of the questions. Make sure each pair gets a chance to share.

CHAPTER 8

The Giver

Director: Phillip Noyce
Newsfront
Rabbit-Proof Fence
Dead Calm
Sliver
The Bone Collector
Patriot Games
Clear and Present Danger

Easter Eggs:
— Nelson Mandela died while the film was being made, and his image is used as one of the "memories" as a tribute.
— The wrist birthmark in the movie is a change from the book, where "light eyes" are the mark of those who can see beyond.
— In the book, Jonas and Fiona don't have a romantic relationship so clearly defined.

Music: Marco Beltrami (also a voice actor in *I, Robot* and the *Scream* series)
Tuesdays With Morrie
Scream (1, 2, 3, 4)
World War Z
Ben Hur
A Quiet Place (Parts I and II)
Academy Award nominations for:
3:10 to Yuma
The Hurt Locker

Characters:
The Giver: Jeff Bridges
The Receiver (Jonas): Brenton Thwaites
Chief Elder: Meryl Streep
Rosemary: Taylor Swift
Jonas' Mother: Katie Holmes
Lily: Emma Tremblay
Jonas' Father: Alexander Skarsgard
Asher: Cameron Monaghan
Fiona: Odeya Rush

DOI: 10.4324/9781003301790-8

I've had mixed feelings about including *The Giver* movie in this book because a very big part of what I've done with Project Based Learning over the years has been based on the Lois Lowry novel, which is included in *The Flexible ELA Classroom*. I decided to include it because I've used it in conjunction with the novel and have always thought it would make a good stand-alone unit. The movie has many changes from the book, but the premise is the same, and it can provide an excellent basis for important conversations in the classroom. I'm going to have the opportunity to try out the movie as a stand-alone this spring, as "pandemic teaching" has caused all of my units to stretch way beyond our typical timeline. Though I'd like to read the novel together with my eighth graders, we are up against state assessments, spring break, and final exams. Simply put: using the movie to facilitate the conversations shaves off at least three weeks from my plans.

Are these ideal teaching conditions? Definitely not. However, I'm convinced that teachers have created quality learning experiences for students throughout many other inopportune circumstances. The other reason I chose this movie is because now, more than any other time in my decades-spanning career, I feel that students are longing for community and are faced with a world right now that is defined by Difference rather than Sameness.

When the Chief Elder, played flawlessly by Meryl Streep, explains that the world was a violent, angry, dissatisfied place with war, starvation, and division caused by "Difference," I get chills. The Chief Elder is barely a passing mention in the book, but is a brilliant addition to the movie to ensure that the viewer is able to understand the reasons why Sameness—a world where there is enough for everyone; everyone has a family, a dwelling, a job chosen based on their talents; and violence and hunger are things of the past—would seem like the perfect solution to the turmoil in the real world.

The movie also does an amazing job revealing all of the beauty in the world that Jonas, the Receiver of Memory, had never experienced because of Sameness. Color, for one, but also music, dancing, and love. Shot in black and white to begin, the viewer discovers color as Jonas does, and the impact is powerful. What we take for granted becomes clear, and for teenagers, the simple things are often overlooked. The movie appeals to teenagers in its addition of several action sequences, a teen romance, and a definite nod to teenagers' distrust of adults who are lying to them. An "us versus them" mentality is revealed as the fate of the future hangs in the balance when it is up to Jonas and Fiona to pull back the veil and reveal a more complex world.

The beauty is that the more complex world is our reality, and this movie experience allows for a rich conversation about the complications of Difference, but also the great dangers of Sameness. To be honest, this movie is going to allow important conversations about the future that are very difficult to have right now. The students in our classrooms are the future adults who will make crucial decisions that are very much about choosing Difference over Sameness, a decision that will impact all of us. If you think this sounds like I'm an alarmist or putting too much credence in these conversations, I'd simply say that I'd rather err on the side of difficult conversations and critical thinking than assuming our students aren't able to talk about important things.

The Pre-Viewing Guide sets up the focal points for students. By asking them to focus on particular categories, it will, in turn, draw their attention to topics the movie addresses. In the decades I've taught this book, this activity is always fun and gives a really nice insight into the values of the students. One of the really interesting things that happens is that when students are asked to create their own Utopia, they often create living conditions that you might not expect. For example, in the last few years, when my students discuss their Utopian ideas, many opt for a very low-tech world, which was quite surprising for me.

As students watch the movie, I have them take note of the "perfect world" characteristics that they notice. However, as the movie progresses, they will have a chance to reassess their ideas by noting "second glance" observations. This is a really powerful tool that we should all incorporate more often. Students need to understand that their first thought isn't necessarily the best, and that further review often requires students to adjust their viewpoint. I believe we have a professional obligation to help students learn this very important skill if we are ever to hope that our society recalibrates.

The Teacher Stop and Chat guides students to think about the topics that will reappear in the final discussion. The ultimate goal in using this movie is for students to have the realization that our inclinations to limit personal freedoms and choices in order to protect citizens could be with good intention; however, despite anyone's best laid plans, when we move closer to Sameness, there is so much lost that the choice is no longer a valid one. The cultural climate that our students have been growing up in may have some students believing that we should do almost anything for an opportunity to all "get along," but this movie and these discussions can open their eyes to the beauty of choice, freedom, and the beauty of the world around them, despite the complexities.

The Discussion Guide asks students to work in groups and assess their own thought processes. This is a metacognitive activity that sharpens students' ability to critically assess multiple beliefs at one time. The sentence stems are written to guide students through the process of "thinking about their own thinking" that was started with the Student Notes. Now, they are collaborating with their peers, and as they explain their choices with peers, the value of the learning increases. Probably my favorite part of teaching this book/movie is that most of my students have not had conversations on these topics. As eighth graders, they just haven't been exposed to the types of philosophical and ethical decisions that this unit provides.

The one caveat I'll add to this chapter is that if you want to—and not everyone will—this movie can spark some very controversial discussions. There is infanticide and euthanasia, both performed under the guises of kindness, committed by members of the community who do not know what they are doing. Their world view that has been spoonfed to them since birth calls these acts Release, and frames them as a positive. Some years, students really want to explore these questions, and other years they don't—even when I teach this unit very similarly. I don't have an answer as to why the response varies, but in some ways I think it is inevitable. There's frankly a lot of deep conversation around the movie, and eighth graders only have so much capacity.

Finally, I'll share with you what made me include this movie, despite my work with it more in regards to Project Based Learning. I was watching the movie when my husband sat down and started watching with me. He'd never read it or watched the movie, but he knows that I teach it every year. Both my kiddos have read it for school, so my husband has heard about it. As he grew more interested, he said, "Do you think this is true? Would Sameness solve some problems? Could we ever get to this point?" My husband is one of the smartest people I know and definitely the most politically informed of our family. He is constantly presenting our family with moral dilemmas that play themselves out in the media for our dinnertime conversations. The fact that he was able to tune in for a short amount of time and be interested in the philosophical issues it raised was enough for me to include this movie in the book. My hope is that some of you who might not teach novels might find a way to include this movie in your work with students to build their critical thinking, help them address complicated ideas, and be guided by a common desire to improve the future.

Name: _____ Date: _____

Pre-Viewing Guide for *The Giver*

Before we view *The Giver*, we are going to think about the things in our world we'd like to change. Dream big, as you are planning what you think a "perfect world," a Utopia, would be like. This is your chance to create a world that you think would make the greatest number of people happy. Jot down your ideas about each category below. Be prepared to share.

Families:	Schools:	Government:
Community:	Money:	Houses:
Freedom for children:	Freedom for adults:	Technology:
Illness:	Violence:	War:
Food:	Weather:	Careers:

When you are done, highlight THREE areas that would be your priority for your "perfect world."

Name: _____ Date: _____

Teacher Stop and Chat for *The Giver*

TOPIC:	TIMESTAMP:	CHAT:
"I didn't want to be different. Who would?"	02:02:00	What do you think about this statement? Do you think that it is good to be different? What about fitting in? Are these always contradictory?
"Jonas, your turn for feelings."	06:20:00	Do you think this is awkward? Why? Do you share your feelings with your family? Friends?
"Five: You may lie."	00:14:00	What would a world without lies be like? Better? Worse?
"It's red."	00:25:15	What might be the significance of the color red? What do we associate red with? What about apples?
"We need Sameness. Don't you agree?"	00:25:52	What do you think of Sameness? What problems would it eliminate? What problems might it cause?
The morning injections remove emotions	00:34:49	For teenagers, and adults, too, to some degree, emotions are overwhelming. What benefits would there be to be rid of them? What negative results?
"Memories aren't just about the past. . . . They determine our future."	00:39:58	What does the Giver mean by this? Do you think this is true for you? Can you change that? In other words, what control do we have over our future?

Name: _____ Date: _____

Teacher Stop and Chat for *The Giver (continued)*

TOPIC:	TIMESTAMP:	CHAT:
There was tremendous cruelty	00:41:00	Would you eliminate cruelty? Pain? What would you be willing to give up to achieve a world like that?
"I didn't want the wisdom. I didn't want the pain. I wanted my childhood again."	00:49:09	Have you experienced this feeling? Do you ever wish that you could "un-know" something or go back to a time when you still were naive?
"He killed him."	00:55:34	This is arguably the turning point for Jonas. To learn that "Release" is death, not another destination, is too much. What stories do we tell about death? Are they helpful?
"Because if you can't feel, what's the point?"	00:56:12	Jonas now believes this, even after he's seen the worst of humanity. Do you think he's right? Or, do you think a better world could exist without all of our emotions?
"Friends forever, right?"	01:10:25	This comment from Fiona to Asher sets up a scene that is coming up. Do you think that they were all three actual friends? Why or why not?
Ceremony of Loss for Jonas	01:12:44	Why do they have a Ceremony of Loss for Jonas? What does it accomplish in terms of keeping things the Same?
The memories return	01:27:26	What do you think happens next? Would it be possible for a Community of Sameness to handle the truth?

Name: _____ Date: _____

Student Notes for *The Giver*

As you view *The Giver*, take note of the things you think are "perfect" at first glance about their world in the left column. Then, if you change your mind, note why in the right column. Teachers: at the end of the movie, before discussion, have students look at the list of "Perfect" characteristics and note in the right column their "second thoughts" after finishing the movie.

"Perfect" characteristics of Sameness	Second thoughts

Name: _____ Date: _____

Discussion Guide for *The Giver*

After allowing students to complete their viewing notes and reflect on the movie, break students into small groups. Have them keep their notes handy, as they will be filling out the following statements together.

Directions: With your group, complete the following statements. Then, be prepared to share how your "second glance" informed your new opinion. Complete three of the following statements. The first one is done for you.

At first, <u>Sameness</u> seems like a good idea, but that was before <u>we realized that taking away Difference would make the world very boring.</u> Then, it became clear that <u>Sameness</u> would lead to a <u>world that may be without prejudice, but it would also not allow for love.</u>

- At first, _____ seems like a good idea, but that was before _____ _____. Then, it became clear that _____ _____ would lead to _____ _____.

- At first, _____ seems like a good idea, but that was before _____ _____. Then, it became clear that _____ _____ would lead to _____ _____.

- At first, _____ seems like a good idea, but that was before _____ _____. Then, it became clear that _____ _____ would lead to _____ _____.

CHAPTER 9

Dear Evan Hansen

Director: Stephen Chbosky
Wonder
Imaginary Friend
The Perks of Being a Wallflower

Easter Eggs:
— "Anybody Have a Map" and "Good for You" were cut from the movie as full songs, but both were used as pep rally songs played by the band.
— *Turtles All the Way Down* by John Green, a book about mental illness, can be seen in the background in a library scene.
— *Ready Player One* is also a book that is prominently displayed.
— Evan has posters for Ben Folds and Radiohead in his room.

Music: Benjamin Pasek and Justin Paul (a songwriting duo)
A Christmas Story
Dogfight
James and the Giant Peach
The Greatest Showman

Characters:
Evan Hansen: Ben Platt
Jared: Nick Dodani
Evan's Mom: Julianne Moore
Connor Murphy: Colton Ryan
Alana: Amandla Stenberg
Larry: Danny Pino
Cynthia: Amy Adams
Zoe: Kaitlyn Denver

DOI: 10.4324/9781003301790-9

To begin, let me say that I was thoroughly unprepared for the original stage version of this musical. I had heard that it was a musical about teens. I had heard it was a musical about suicide. I knew it had been immediately canonized by critics and regular theater-goers alike. What I didn't know is that I would sob uncontrollably with a theater of strangers, while they also sobbed uncontrollably. There was a moment toward the end when the sounds of our collective breathing seemed to be a part of the show itself. To say that I love the musical *Dear Evan Hansen* is a giant understatement.

So, when the movie version was released with a now 27-year-old Ben Platt reprising his role, I was shocked by how much some people seemed to hate it. Some hated it because Ben was far too old to play a 17-year-old. Others hated it because they simply loved the musical too much to make room in their hearts and minds for any other version. At first I couldn't decide if I wanted to see it or not. But, it was 2021, and I was a long year into mostly being quarantined, so when I was able to go to the movies, I did.

The movie is good. Better than good, actually, but it just won't touch live theater; however, I think it is crucial to include this movie here because everyone deserves to see it and experience it, even if the movie can't live up to live theater. After all, I don't know anyone who has ever made the argument that a movie version of a theater production can even truthfully be compared. Yet, the movie itself, as a stand-alone, artistic endeavor is deeply moving, well acted, and timely.

What struck me most while watching the movie is how this amazing story is now readily accessible to the general population. It is a mark of privilege to have "theater tickets," an opportunity that so many of our students do not have, and it is for them that I include the movie version of *Dear Evan Hansen*. I would not show this movie to a middle school class, even though I know for a fact that many of them are obsessed. The same is true of productions like *Hamilton*—the content is just a tad more mature than my eighth graders, and nothing can ruin powerful moments more quickly than a room of pubescent boys who think they are funny. (Of course I generalize, but it comes from two decades of experience.)

However, I would definitely show this as early as ninth grade. I don't know how to explain it, but there is a world of difference between middle and high school, so much so that I'd be 100% comfortable showing this to any high school class. I would consider a "trigger warning" and make the class aware that the movie deals with suicide, but much more, the aftermath of those left behind than the suicide itself. Students are already familiar with the premise of the movie, so if any student is uncomfortable, you can direct them to one of the alternate assignments in the appendixes. I don't typically have students who opt out of a movie, especially at the high school level, but just in case, it is better to be prepared.

The central purpose of teaching this movie is to provide hope for struggling students. Every day there are students in our classes who are just barely hanging on. Every day there are students who are incredibly lonely. Every day there are students who are invisible. This movie provides the chance to talk about these very taboo topics in an acceptable way—about the characters in a story and not about themselves. The goal, of course, is to create classroom communities that are capable of accepting students as they are, mental health issues and all.

Sit back for a moment here and indulge me. More than any other belief that I hold about what is good for students, I believe that being a part of a classroom community is crucial, and that is because I have seen daily, for my entire teaching career, students struggle alone with their mental health. Now, things have changed quite a bit. I'd say a good quarter of my students see a counselor or therapist, and they talk about mental health without fear. Another quarter are medicated in some way. Yet, here we are, still trying to handle the taboo topic of mental health.

I grew up in a household that did not believe in talking to therapists. In fact, when an astute guidance counselor noticed my depression in fifth grade, she called my home. My mom was very kind, but basically told her I was just "dramatic." My dad warned me to never, ever bring up "family business" to anyone. He made me feel that I was weak for letting my guard down, letting anyone know that I was not strong enough to handle my business myself. I struggled throughout my middle and high school years, and finally when I went to college, I was able to find a therapist and medication to help me find some balance. My own children cannot imagine a household like the one I grew up in. I try to explain that it was a different time, and mental health wasn't taught in health classes or really discussed at all. There was a stigma that clung to anyone who needed mental health help.

Things have obviously improved, but I believe that mental health is the last great taboo in our society. In my lifetime, I have watched with excitement as gay marriage became legal, trans rights became codified in law, and gender has become more about a continuum than a prescription. Despite these major accomplishments as a society, we are not comfortable confronting another frontier: our own mental well-being.

We've made what I like to call "window dressing progress." What I mean by that is that so many of us talk about taking a "mental health day," where our colleagues imagine that we've taken a long bath and curled up with a good book and a cup of coffee. This is the window dressing. It's easy to talk about it like that, right? It "looks" right. However, many of us, when we take a "mental health day," are on couches crying, letting dishes pile up and laundry go unfolded because, for whatever reason, on that day, we hit a wall. For lack of a better description, there are times when so many of us just reach an "I just can't" crisis, and instead of being able to speak our truth honestly, we rely on the "window dressing" progress we've made to sort of, kind of, in a roundabout way, say to our colleagues that we are having a hard time.

What if we were actually allowed to tell our boss that we are struggling without fear of repercussions? For the first 15 years of my career, I never once mentioned any of my mental health challenges. Why? My dad was in my ear, in my head, reminding me that I couldn't look weak. My dad always made sure that we all knew how to handle our business, whatever that may be. He did not think his requests of us were unreasonable because it was the same way he lived his life. He got stuff done. I'm proud of my stoicism, when I can keep that facade going. However, I'm no longer worried that my colleagues will think less of me for my challenges. Instead, I try to be an example to my colleagues and my students by being open about seeing a therapist, taking medication, and living in a constant battle to fight off demons that are able to convince me that I am too weak to pursue my dreams.

This may seem wildly personal to you, and if it does, I'm glad to make you uncomfortable, as that truly is the first step in changing our culture and our classrooms. We must be willing to simply allow, without judgment, others to express themselves and fill those awkward spaces with acceptance of one another. The movie does an amazing job of capturing the awkwardness that comes with genuine expression of self, particularly when that expression isn't positive. The characters must work through their emotions, and there are moments that are painful to experience vicariously.

I'd also note that the conversations I planned for this chapter aren't particularly about suicide, though the pandemic has made this a more important topic than ever, as suicide rates are rising. The conversations are instead about emotion, how we perceive ourselves, how we perceive others, and the way our actions can have a huge ripple effect. These are seemingly safer topics, but I'll warn you that most students have a layer of hurt right beneath the surface that may be revealed. If that happens, encourage your students to be honest, respectful, and perhaps go over some ground rules for personal conversations. I always present our class as our "community" and discuss what is and isn't acceptable in our community. For example, one rule that I established early is not to dismiss anyone's feelings. It is very common when someone says they are doing poorly to just point out how much they have to be thankful for, when in reality that approach is rather dismissive. Instead, we must hold space for one another, which is just another way of framing our reactions. We must simply be there for one another, supporting but not trying to solve all the problems.

The Pre-Viewing Guide touches on many high school tropes. We spend time learning about tropes, and why authors and directors use them. The easy answer is that they are relatable. The deeper answer is that tropes speak to the universal, and good art, whether it be a novel or a movie, brings our experiences into focus, helping us to locate ourselves within the human drama. In other words, just as the song says, "you will be found."

The Student Notes sheet allows students a great deal of freedom in their notetaking. Generally, this movie is best watched with fewer disruptions than the others so far, and you'll notice that the "Teacher Stop and Chat" has fewer moments where the teacher directs the experience of the movie. Mostly, the movie is the vehicle by which we will arrive at the final discussion, which is pretty intense. Students need to be able to have difficult conversations with each other, but also an opportunity to learn about themselves and bring their introspection into focus as a part of a classroom community.

Name: _____ Date: _____

Pre-Viewing Guide for *Dear Evan Hansen*

Before we begin the movie version of *Dear Evan Hansen*, we need to understand its use of tropes. Tropes are common conventions in a particular medium, used often enough that they are recognizable. In other words, a trope is a commonplace, recognizable element that conveys bigger meaning. Every genre has some. Let's explore some tropes that you'll likely recognize. Leave the last column blank until after you watch the movie.

TROPE:	EXAMPLES:	YOUR THOUGHTS:	*DEAR EVAN HANSEN:*
Protagonist is in love with their best friend			
Dark or bad characters wear black			
Parents just don't understand			
First love equals true love			
Reluctant hero			
Sidekicks are for comic relief			

With your group, brainstorm an answer to these questions:
What purpose do tropes serve in movies?
Why might a director choose to use a well-known trope?
What does it accomplish when the audience has the same understanding?

Name: _____ Date: _____

Teacher Stop and Chat for *Dear Evan Hansen*

TOPIC:	TIMESTAMP:	CHAT:
"Dear Evan Hansen, . . ."	01:25:00	The movie starts with Evan writing a letter to himself. This serves as an interior monologue, a way for the viewer to understand what Evan is thinking. Is this effective? What does it reveal, right away?
"I wish everything was different."	00:12:23	Evan is obviously struggling. Have you ever wished that "everything was different"? Isn't this a part of growing up? What makes it seem worse to Evan?
"His last words . . ."	00:18:45	Evan allows Connor's parents to believe what they want to about the letter they found. Is this kind or ultimately cruel? Or, did Evan even think about it at all? Was it just his social anxiety that allowed this to happen?
"No requiem."	00:41:18	The tragedy, of course, is the suicide. However, there is another layer to the trauma. Both Zoe and Connor's dad didn't have a positive relationship, and therefore don't know how to grieve. How might they feel guilty for not feeling grief? (They have "no requiem," which is an act of remembrance.)
Zoe: "Your mom has probably never been rich then." *Evan: "Yeah, you've probably never been poor."*	00:47:59	Evan and Zoe face the awkward realization that they each think they have it worse than the other. What problems might the rich have that the poor wouldn't understand? What problems might the poor have that the rich wouldn't understand?

TOPIC:	TIMESTAMP:	CHAT:
"I'm glad you're here."	00:54:18	Contrast the way that Connor's family has welcomed him in versus how Evan's own mom is so busy working. Is it fair for Evan to resent his mom for having to work? Is there anything wrong with finding other people to act as family?
"You're, you know . . . and, I, um, am not." *"You don't act like a depressed sort of person."*	00:55:36	How are we sometimes like Evan in our inability to see that we are more alike than different? Why can't he believe that Alana would take medication for depression and anxiety?

Name: _____ Date: _____.

Teacher Stop and Chat for *Dear Evan Hansen (continued)*

TOPIC:	TIMESTAMP:	CHAT:
"The parts we can't tell, we carry them well, but that doesn't mean they aren't heavy."	00:59:43	Alana's anxiety looks very different from Evan's. How might we begin looking at others with an appreciation of "what they carry" versus what we see them dealing with? Do we ever tend to downplay others' struggles? Why might we do that?
Reverberation	01:05:04	A microphone reverberating, or giving feedback, is a well-known trope. What does it suggest to you, even if you knew nothing about what Evan was going to say?
"Lift your head and look around, you will be found."	01:09:29	This is the most well-known song of the musical. Why does the song go viral? What resonates with you about the song?
"So, speaking of scholarships . . ."	01:29:17	Evan's mom is humiliated and furious that Connor's family wants to offer him a scholarship. Why do you think so?
"Just to know that we're somehow not alone."	01:36:30	Even though the Connor project is based in a lie, do you see the value in everyone coming together around a common cause? Or does it diminish the end result? If you had contributed money or shared a story, how might you feel to find out the truth?
"I'd rather pretend I'm something better than these broken parts."	01:48:02	Evan's breakthrough moment of truly understanding the significance of his actions occurs at the tree he "fell" out of before school started. Why do you think this is important? What does it tell us about him?
"I wanted to be sure that you saw this. He really loved it here."	02:06:15	Zoe meets Evan at the orchard. What do you think this choice signals about her feelings? How does it provide closure for the characters and the viewers?

Name: _____ Date: _____.

Student Notes for *Dear Evan Hansen*

Instead of traditional notes, you will leave "notes" in each of the following characters' lockers. The "notes" can be advice, quotes, warnings, or simply your opinions. Try to be as authentic as possible. Feel free to use shorthand or "texting" abbreviations and to include artwork as well.

Dear Connor,
Dear Evan,
Dear Zoe,
Dear Jared,

Name: _____ Date: _____.

Discussion Guide for *Dear Evan Hansen*

After viewing the movie, you will write a brief "review." The movie received many bad reviews, only achieving around 30% on Rotten Tomatoes by critics, but an 88% audience score. Rate the following categories from 1 to 10, with 10 being the highest. Write one sentence after each category that encapsulates your feelings. You'll be sharing and defending your review in our class discussion.

Cast:

1   2   3   4   5   6   7   8   9   10

_____

_____

Music:

1   2   3   4   5   6   7   8   9   10

_____

_____

Plot:

1   2   3   4   5   6   7   8   9   10

_____

_____

Relatability:

1   2   3   4   5   6   7   8   9   10

_____

_____

Accurate depiction of teenagers:

1   2   3   4   5   6   7   8   9   10

_____

_____

Treatment of mental illness:

1   2   3   4   5   6   7   8   9   10

_____

_____

CHAPTER 10

The Social Dilemma

Director: Jeff Orlowski
Chasing Ice
Chasing Coral

Easter Eggs:
—Cassandra could be a reference to the Greek character who had the gift of prophecy, but the curse of never being believed.
—Chris Messina (who invented the hashtag is in a crowd scene).

Music: Mark Crawford
Chasing Ice
Chasing Coral
The Love Bug

Characters:
Tristan Harris
Ben: Skyler Gisondo
Jaron Lanier
Cassandra: Kara Hayward
Tim Kendall
Artificial Intelligence: Vincent Kartheiser
Isla: Sophia Hammond
Justin Rosenstein
Anna Lembke
Shoshana Zuboff
Rebecca: Catalina Garayoa
Mom: Barbara Gehring
Stepdad: Chris Grundy

I had no intention of including a documentary-drama in this book, but I'm staring down the last quarter of this school year with fear and trepidation. Everything has been so difficult, right? My students haven't had the stamina to move at the "normal" pace, there's been an incredible uptick in mental health issues, and there's a weird pressure for my students to somehow do well on a final exam that was designed for pre-pandemic times. Between COVID and quarantining, I have a decent number of students who have missed weeks of school. This school year has been interminable and has also passed ridiculously quickly.

So, here I am. I'm going to have to begin reviewing for my final exam way earlier than ever before to ensure that my students do well. This leaves me with some time, but not enough time to do an entire novel unit or a full-blown writing assignment. I started thinking about this time crunch and realized that I wanted to end my students' eighth grade year with something that was both highly engaging and powerful for them as they move on to high school. Though I considered all of the movies in the book for the final unit, and I almost settled on a few of the choices, I realized that there was a conversation that I needed to have with these students in particular that would need the structure of a new movie unit.

This all hits quite close to home, as I have an eighth grader. He's suffered greatly from the pandemic, particularly since he was fully virtual for his seventh grade year. Isolation hit him hard, and the lack of social interactions caused an incredible amount of stress this school year. We've had a love/hate relationship with social media, as it was both a lifeline and a pit of quicksand, simultaneously. Just like any other parent of eighth graders, I questioned his reliance on social media, but it was all a bit twisted, as I was teaching online, keeping up with my friends online, and even having a horrific family meeting of my five brothers and sisters with my hospitalized dad as he slipped in and out of consciousness, all while a sweet nurse was holding an iPad up for him. To say that my relationship with social media and technology has become complicated is an understatement. I vacillate between wanting to chuck it all and embrace some Walden-esque lifestyle and wanting to share everything I write with the entire world.

The conversation that I propose for your classroom, as it is the one that I will be having this spring, is more of an inquiry. I am certainly poised as a facilitator of this conversation rather than an expert, as I am certain I don't have the answers. I've struggled with "technology" all year—technology meaning anything that is computerized or internet related. I've done webinars on how to unplug and give students a break, all while understanding the irony of doing a webinar about unplugging. I've recognized that some tools are simply too good to ever give up. EdPuzzle, Blooket, and the entire Google Suite are non-negotiably a part of how I will teach going forward. The results that my students were able to produce in the midst of the pandemic with these tools is evidence enough that they are valuable.

On the other hand, prior to the pandemic, there were recommendations about screen time that we've all had to simply ignore in order to operate in a world of Zoom calls, online classes, and virtual birthday parties. It is as if our pre-pandemic selves and our current iterations cannot co-exist. This tension is what has led me to include *The Social Dilemma* as the final movie of this book. I need to work out these thoughts and feelings *with* my students if I am ever going to understand how the future of school should look. I have some students who thrived online, others who completely tanked, and many who simply showed up, which, unfortunately, was all we could ask in many circumstances.

The Pre-Viewing Guide is crucial to set the stage. Students will shut down if they suspect that this unit is being taught by another adult who doesn't understand their world trying to tell them how to live in it. I need to come at this humbly, as an adult who isn't sure of the answers, even though I pride myself on my own social media savvy. Truth be told, students always have and always will have a leg up on adults when it comes to what's new. However, I've been talking about social media with my college students in my Canisius College class called "Adolescent Literacy in a New Literacy World." We look at all the literacies our world requires: digital, media, data, health, news, coding and computational, visual, technological, financial, ethical, civic, and even gaming literacy. In all our conversations, however, we always seem to return to social media. I've asked why that is their entry point into so many other literacies, and their answers have been enlightening. One student recently summed it up well: "Almost everything we learn outside of school is via social media, in one form or another." As teachers, we need to consider the tremendous role that social media plays in our students' lives and tread carefully.

The Student Notes sheet is meant to help students ask the right questions. It is important for teachers to let this unit be student driven, so allowing them to formulate their own questions is central to the success of the entire unit. The note sheet is basic, but it will help students organize their thoughts. You can use the questions they generate to start or end class on the days that you are viewing the movie.

The Teacher Stop and Chat focuses students on the specific issues that the movie addresses while also personalizing it. The one area of CASEL's Competencies that is often hard to address is that of *Social Awareness*. As a middle school teacher, it is often simply too much to ask of students to think outside of themselves into the realm of "other." However, this movie provides an entry point into larger conversations about the world around them. The best part of this unit is going to be the fact that many students are unaware of the lure of the internet and the addictive properties of social media as it relates to others. I've never had a conversation with any teen who is unaware of the power of their phone over them. They readily admit addiction, but they stop there. They are not aware of the issue as a global problem, and this is an important conversation for students to have as they consider their place in the world.

Finally, the Discussion Guide brings it all together. The goal of the final discussion is a good, old-fashioned "spitballing" session where students propose solutions to the nagging issues that the movie brings up. I don't want to leave students hopeless as they finish the school year, but rather, they should leave the discussion empowered with a list of actionable steps that will help them navigate the complexities of "technology."

Even though this is the last chapter of the book, that doesn't necessarily mean that this is the last unit you'd do with students. In fact, I can easily see this unit being a beginning of the year starting point as a part of a Digital Literacy or Digital Citizenship unit. I feel that students would be engaged right away by being asked their opinions on topics that are meaningful to them. It could also pave the way for other units in the book. For example, I'd imagine that students would be able to easily connect the dots of a digital "Big Brother" here with the Sameness prescribed in *The Giver* or the complex relationship that we have with technology in *The Mitchells vs. The Machines*. I'm hopeful that including this chapter provides a way for educators to engage students while helping equip them with some of the necessary tools for analyzing and perhaps modifying their behaviors.

I do have a final thought about this chapter that I'd be remiss if I didn't voice. There's a tremendous amount of hypocrisy, at least for me, in telling students how to manage technology, since I'm struggling with it myself. As I mentioned, I vacillate between a great exorcism from all things social media and a terrific desire to connect with teachers around the world about the rollercoaster experience of being a teacher. Perhaps the greatest lesson I can provide for students is that my relationship with technology is ever-changing and evolving. If you find yourself in the same boat as me, I'd like to recommend that we are all honest with the next generation.

Maybe we didn't know how addictive it was when we handed our two-year-olds educational iPad games. Maybe we didn't understand that just because everyone else's kiddo had a cell phone in fourth grade didn't mean it was a good idea. I find that owning up to my lack of understanding that set the stage for today's technology crisis is appreciated by those who are dealing with the repercussions. My mind keeps coming back to the tired, but certainly appropriate, name for teachers: Lead Learners. May we all be willing to embrace our role as Lead Learners, facilitating meaningful experiences for our students and ourselves.

Name: _____ Date: _____

Pre-Viewing Guide for *The Social Dilemma*

Do NOT put your name on this sheet. Answer each question honestly. We will be discussing the answers, but without knowing whose answers we are viewing.

1. How many texts do you imagine you send a day?
2. How many hours do you spend per day on social media?
3. Do you use your real name on social media?
4. Do you have any "private stories" or accounts that are hidden?
5. How many of the people who you follow do you actually know in person?
6. How many of the people who you follow would you be willing to meet in real life?
7. How many times do you think you check your phone during the school day?
8. Do you sleep with your phone nearby?
9. Do you ever feel bad about yourself after being on social media?
10. If there was one thing adults needed to know about social media, what would it be?

*Have students crumple up this page and have a "snowball fight." Have them pick up other snowballs they see on the ground and throw them, too. After about a minute, have students pick up a "snowball" and uncrumple the paper. Take turns having students read the answers to the first question and discuss. Repeat throwing "snowballs" for each question.

Name: _____ Date: _____

Teacher Stop and Chat for *The Social Dilemma*

TOPIC:	TIMESTAMP:	CHAT:
"I mean, there were meaningful, systemic changes happening around the world because of these platforms that were positive."	02:39:00	What are the positives of social media, as you experience them? Think about the platforms you use regularly.
"What is the problem?"	03:28:00	Why do you think all of these insiders have a hard time answering this question? What do you think? What is the problem?
*"If you're not paying for the product, **then you are the product**."*	00:13:20	What does this mean? Do you pay for any of the social media platforms that you use?
"Good idea. GPS coordinates indicate that they're in close proximity."	00:20:48	Were you aware that your location is used to determine what ads you receive and how a platform interacts with you? How does that make you feel?
". . . Activating ellipsis."	00:26:09	What is the impact of the ellipsis when you see it on the screen? What does it cause you to do?
"If something is not a tool, it's demanding things from you."	00:30:22	By this definition, is the internet a tool? Is your phone a tool?
"If it's not that big a deal, then don't use it for a week."	00:36:59	How would you fare? Could you go a week without any social media at all?

TOPIC:	TIMESTAMP:	CHAT:
"But were we evolved to be aware of what 10,000 people think of us?"	00:39:02	Can you actually conceptualize 10,000 people? How can we allow ourselves to be manipulated by a concept that most of us can't even truly understand?
Digital pacifier	00:43:31	Do you think that your phone is a digital pacifier? Think of it like a baby pacifier. Do you, when you start to feel bored, anxious, uncomfortable, etc., want to look at your phone?
Artificial Intelligence	00:48:01	Were you aware how much AI is already "out there"? Does this make you nervous? Or, does the convenience and ease of our life make AI necessary?

Name: _____ Date: _____

Teacher Stop and Chat for *The Social Dilemma (continued)*

TOPIC:	TIMESTAMP:	CHAT:
Wikipedia	00:55:15	What would be the impact of Wikipedia being adaptable to our own interests? How could we agree on anything if we all viewed something different?
Echo chamber	00:56:47	When you are only hearing and seeing those in your feed who agree with you, it creates an echo chamber. This means that you are not getting the whole story. How does that impact you?
"The algorithms are trying to find which rabbit hole is closest to your interest."	00:59:54	Do you have a "rabbit hole" that you tend to go down? This can be a super specialized topic or a general one. Its only goal is to make you go to another link or site and keep going.
Fake news on Twitter spreads six times faster than true news	01:02:17	Why do you think this is true? Have you ever fallen victim to believing something you later found out wasn't true?
Extreme content	01:06:01	Do you ever find yourself interested in the news or information that is extreme? How can you determine if this content is helpful or hurtful to you?

TOPIC:	TIMESTAMP:	CHAT:
"Now, imagine what that means in the hands of a dictator or an authoritarian."	01:06:50	How might someone use the addictiveness of social media for evil or bad purposes? How can you protect yourself from this?
"It's as though we have less and less control over who we are and what we believe."	01:09:12	Does this oversimplify things? Don't we have autonomy over what we put into our brains? Or, are we up against something bigger?
Culture wars	01:14:09	Do you believe that the damage of culture wars can be undone? If so, can social media be used for good? Can your generation change the narrative?
"It's the ability of technology to bring out the worst in society . . ."	01:18:07	Do you think this is true? Have you seen technology used to bring out the best in society as well? Is it just an extreme medium?
Humane technology	01:26:00	Knowing what you know now, do you think that humane technology can be created? Can humans change the chaos that technology has turned into?

Name: _____ Date: _____

Student Notes for *The Social Dilemma*

As you watch, jot down questions that you have about each of the four topics provided. Be as specific as possible, as we'll use these questions to debrief after the movie.

Privacy:	Addiction:
Laws:	**Monetization:**

Name: _____ Date: _____

The Social Dilemma Discussion Guide

This movie is thought provoking and could easily leave us feeling helpless about addictions to technology, the monetization of our data, the lack of laws and oversight, and the loss of privacy. Instead of being "stuck" with this situation, you are going to work with your group to propose solutions to these issues. Go back to your Student Notes sheet and discuss the questions that you have. Then, propose some ideas that would improve our relationship with social media and technology.

We submit the following proposals regarding PRIVACY:
We submit the following proposals regarding LAWS:
We submit the following proposals regarding ADDICTION:
We submit the following proposals regarding MONETIZATION:

Be ready to share your findings with the class. We'll be creating a single Google Doc that combines our best ideas, and we'll share our thoughts with Exposure Labs, the production company.

CHAPTER 11

Keep Connecting

The day before New Year's Eve, my 16-year-old daughter and I spent a few hours at the Well-Now Emergency Clinic. No COVID. No strep. She was "just sick." We were thankful for this, but when we began discussing how she had to cancel her plans for New Year's Eve, she exploded into a crying mess. This wasn't a big party. This was a sleepover with three friends. When I pressed her—explaining that she could have them over the next week—she said something that is going to define how I "do school" during this crisis. She said, "You know how when we were little, you always told us what was coming next? Like, the next thing to look forward to? Well, there's not that much to look forward to, so the little things like this is what I've got right now."

As my students and I begin the next segment of the pandemic, I'm going to keep this view in mind. The fact is, Zoey's right. There's not that much to look forward to because there is so much uncertainty. I need to give my students more in-the-moment support, surprises, and accolades. My co-teacher and I are trying to bring a little more joy in their day to day. For example, I have two couches in my room. Instead of randomly assigning students, we decided that we'd have "Students of the Week" for each period. Each student got a couch for the week, based on a random-ish compliment we gave them. They could keep the couch to themselves or invite a friend to sit with them. One week's "compliment couch" winners heard what we noticed or liked about them. Sydney had been out of school for two weeks, yet had gotten a 100 on a test because she emailed us to stay up to date. Adri was always smiling under her mask and nodding encouragingly at us when we taught. Troy always said goodbye when he left. I had witnessed McKenzie being really nice to a student who was having a bad day. Carol helped translate when we got a new student who spoke no English. Students were appropriately bashful and embarrassed as we announced these achievements like Emmy nominations, but they LOVED this corny reward.

DOI: 10.4324/9781003301790-11

In addition to our "compliment couch" plan, my co-teacher is a huge sports fan. She began each period today with trivia, and rewarded students who knew the answer with candy. These two things were small, yet there was a difference in my room in the course of just a few days. We are planning to deliberately spread joy not by the big things we do, but instead by the ways we help our students feel a part of our unique community, and we plan to keep connecting with our students. Of course we laugh because no one was that appreciative when we allowed students to remediate and retake their last test! We look forward to the days when it isn't quite as hard to find something to look forward to, but I think this newest lesson in pandemic teaching is worth remembering.

Appendix A
Movie Permission Slips

Name: _____ Date: _____

Dear families and caregivers,

Do you have a favorite movie? Do you have a scene that you can quote word for word? Almost everyone does, right? This is why we'll be using films in our classroom this year. *Movie Magic* is real! Sometimes the best way to engage with students and deepen their connections with content and each other is through a film, and for this reason I am asking your permission for your child to watch the following films this year:

Inside Out (PG)

Big Hero Six (PG)

Encanto (PG)

Wreck-It Ralph (PG)

Soul (PG)

Wonder (PG)

Hidden Figures (PG)

We will not be watching all of these, but a pre-signed permission slip allows me to make adjustments quickly. These films are PG, but I want to assure you that as a parent and teacher, these films are not just to pass time, but contain important connections to content and social emotional learning. I am privileged to view them with your child and guide them through their meaning.

Please sign below, indicating your permission. If you do not grant your permission, I'll be in contact about planning an alternate assignment for your child. I'm super excited to share *Movie Magic* with your kiddo!

_____

Your name: _____   Child's name: _____

❏ Yes, my child may watch the movies above.
❏ No, my child may not watch the movies above. Please contact me at
    _____ to plan an alternate assignment.

Name: _____ Date: _____

Dear families and caregivers,

Do you have a favorite movie? Do you have a scene that you can quote word for word? Almost everyone does, right? This is why we'll be using films in our classroom this year. *Movie Magic* is real! Sometimes the best way to engage with students and deepen their connections with content and each other is through a film, and for this reason I am asking your permission for your child to watch the following films this year:

Inside Out (PG)

Big Hero Six (PG)

Encanto (PG)

Wreck-It Ralph (PG)

Soul (PG)

Wonder (PG)

Hidden Figures (PG)

The Perks of Being A Wallflower (PG-13)

The Hate You Give (PG-13)

Love, Simon (PG-13)

We will not be watching all of these, but a pre-signed permission slip allows me to make adjustments quickly. There are several that are PG-13, but the content is appropriate and is not outside the types of topics your child would reference in health class and see on social media daily. As a parent and teacher, I want to assure you that these films have value, and my job will be to navigate them with your child.

Please sign below, indicating your permission. If you do not grant your permission, I'll be in contact about planning an alternate assignment for your child. I'm super excited to share *Movie Magic* with your kiddo!

_____

Your name: _____ Child's name: _____

❏ Yes, my child may watch the movies above.
❏ No, my child may not watch the movies above. Please contact me at _____ to plan an alternate assignment.

Appendix B
Alternate Assignments

For students who are not watching the movie

Using a book that you've read, choose tasks from this chart to complete a tic-tac-toe. You may do these tasks on poster board and paper or digitally.

Think of a book that you've read where the ending just didn't "sit right" with you. Maybe it felt unfinished, or maybe it felt out of character. Write a final chapter of the book that will make it feel more realistic or relatable to you.	Create a cast list for your favorite book and make the movie poster. Make sure to include the title, a quote or two from the book, and pictures of all the characters. Make it appealing to the audience and intrigue them into coming to the movie.	Make a storyboard of the major events of the novel. Include at least eight plot points with either pictures and/or symbols.
Express, in a series of social media posts, the experience of one of the characters in the book. Be sure to include pictures. Then, on the opposite side, create a series of reaction posts by the other characters.	Organize a list of symbols, one for each character. Make a visual representation of the symbols and how they connect. Use at least eight symbols.	Integrate yourself into the book! Write a series of conversations or a scene with you in the book. How would you either fit right in or disrupt the story arc? Are you the new protagonist or an antagonist?

Organize a road trip for at least three of the characters. Where would they go? What would they pack? What would be their purpose? Include a map.	Express, in a journal entry, the real feelings of one of the characters. This journal will not be read by any of the other characters.	Write a letter to the protagonist or the antagonist. In the letter, offer insights that would help them to come to an epiphany or realization. You may need to provide evidence from the novel to persuade them you are right.

Appendix C
Assessment Choice Board

Make	Organize	Verify	Integrate	Express
Make a map of the setting. It may be on poster board or digital. Make sure to include at least five landmarks and a key, and use color and scale.	Organize a party for the characters in the movie. Include what they are celebrating, where it would take place, the menu, and a budget.	Verify the locations that are used in the movie. Are they real? Imagined? If real, are they accurate? If imagined, are they inspired by a place?	Integrate a new character into the plot of the story. Create a character and write either a series of conversations or a scene with the new character.	Express, in a journal entry, the real feelings of one of the characters. This journal will not be read by any of the other characters.
Make a storyboard of the major events of the movie. Include at least eight plot points with either pictures and/ or symbols.	Organize the movie into an accurate chronological order with at least eight plot points. Label the story arc.	Verify the origin story of the movie. What does the director say? If based on a book, how closely related is it?	Integrate new information into the story. Provide a new fact that would change the outcome for the characters.	Express, in a letter, the real feelings of one of the characters. The other characters will see this letter.

Make	Organize	Verify	Integrate	Express
Make character trading cards. On the front, include a picture and a catchphrase. On the back, include a profile.	Organize a list of symbols, one for each character. Make a visual representation of the symbols and how they connect.	Verify the facts presented in the movie. Check the accuracy of information that is presented. Look at three different aspects.	Integrate a new cast for the movie. Create a list of at least three different cast members and determine the impact on the movie.	Express, in a series of social media posts, the experience of one of the characters in the movie. Be sure to include pictures.
Make an alternate movie poster. Focus on a different aspect than ones that you have seen. Include characters, hints, and quotes.	Organize a road trip for at least three of the characters. Where would they go? What would they pack? What would be their purpose? Include a map.	Verify the time period the movie is set in. Are the details accurate? Is there a time period where the movie would also work well? Does the time period matter?	Integrate yourself into the movie! Write a series of conversations or a scene with you in the movie. How would you either fit right in or disrupt the film?	Express, in a how-to article, the knowledge that one of the characters has about how to do something that is specialized knowledge. You may need research.

Appendix D
Teacher Stop and Chat

TOPIC:	TIMESTAMP:	CHAT:

For Product Safety Concerns and Information please contact our
EU representative GPSR@taylorandfrancis.com Taylor & Francis
Verlag GmbH, Kaufingerstraße 24, 80331 München, Germany